John Pinkerton

Scottish tragic ballads

John Pinkerton

Scottish tragic ballads

ISBN/EAN: 9783742828859

Manufactured in Europe, USA, Canada, Australia, Japa

Cover: Foto ©Angelika Wolter / pixelio.de

Manufactured and distributed by brebook publishing software (www.brebook.com)

John Pinkerton

Scottish tragic ballads

SCOTTISH

TRAGIC BALLADS.

LONDON,
PRINTED BY AND FOR J. NICHOLS.
MDCCLXXXI.

HARDYKNUTE,

AN HEROIC BALLAD,

NOW FIRST PUBLISHED COMPLETE;

WITH THE OTHER MORE APPROVED

SCOTTISH BALLADS,

AND SOME NOT HITHERTO MADE PUBLIC,

IN THE TRAGIC STILE.

TO WHICH ARE PREFIXED

TWO DISSERTATIONS,

I. ON THE ORAL TRADITION OF POETRY.
II. ON THE TRAGIC BALLAD.

JAMQUE SACRUM TENERIS VATEM VENERETUR AB ANNIS.

CONTENTS.

DISSERTATION I.	Page ix
DISSERTATION II.	xxviii
1. *Hardyknute*, Part I.	1
Part II.	16
2. *Child Maurice.*	35
3. *Adam o Gordon.*	43
4. *Sir Hugh, or the Jew's Daughter.*	50
5. *Flodden Field, or the Flowers of the Forest.*	53
6. *Edward.*	54
7. *Sir Patrick Spence.*	57
8. *Lady Bothwell's Lament.*	59
9. *Earl of Murray.*	60
10. *Sir James the Rose.*	61
11. *Laird of Woodhouselie.*	65
12. *Lord Livingston.*	69

13. *Binnorie.*

13. Binnorie.	72
14. Death of Menteith.	75
15. Lord Airth's Complaint.	77
16. "I wish I were where Helen lyes."	79
Fragments.	81
Notes.	87
Glossary.	125

DISSERTATIONS

ON THE

ORAL TRADITION OF POETRY,

AND ON

THE TRAGIC BALLAD.

DISSERTATION I.

ON THE ORAL TRADITION OF POETRY.

IT has long been a subject of regret, that the inventors of the fine Arts have by oblivion been deprived of the reputation due to their memory. Of the many realms which lay claim to their birth, Egypt seems to possess the preference. Yet, like the Nile, which animates that country, while they have diffused pleasure and utility over kingdoms, their origin remains hid in the most profound obscurity.

That poetry holds a distinguished superiority over all these sciences is allowed; yet the first practiser of this enchanting art has lost the renown it was designed to confer. We must either allow the contested claim of the Osiris of the Egyptians, and Apollo of the Greeks, or be content to withhold from any, the fame which indeed seems due to as many inventors as there are distinct nations in the world. For poetry appears not to require the labour of disquisition, or aid of chance, to invent; but is rather the original language of men in an infant state of society in all countries. It is the effusion of fancy actuated by the passions: and that these are always strongest when uncontrouled by custom, and the manners which in an advanced community are termed polite, is evident. But the peculiar advantages, which a certain situation of extrinsic objects confer on this art, have already been so well illustrated by eminent critics *, that it is unnecessary here to remember them. I have besides noted a few such as immediately concern the compositions now under view in the subsequent Dissertation: and only propose here to give a brief account of the utility of the Oral Tradition of Poetry, in that barbarous state of society which necessarily precedes the invention of letters; and of the circumstances that conspired to render it easy and safe.

Among the Egyptians, probably the most ancient authors of the elegant, as well as useful sciences, we find that verses were originally used solely to preserve the laws of their princes, and sayings of their wise men from oblivion †. These were sometimes inscribed in their temples in their hieroglyphic character, but more

---

* Particularly Dr. Blackwell in his Enquiry into the Life and Writings of Homer; and Dr. Blair in his elegant Dissertation on the Poems of Ossian.

† Herodot. Diodor. Sicul. &c.

frequently

frequently only committed to the memory of the expounders of their law, or disciples of their sages. Pythagoras, who was initiated in their secret science, conveyed in like manner his dictates to his disciples, as appears from the moral verses which pass under his name at this day. And though the authenticity of these may be questioned, yet that he followed this mode of bequeathing his knowledge to his followers, is proved from the consent of all antiquity *. Nay, before him, Thales composed in like manner his System of Natural Philosophy. And even so late as the time of Aristotle, the laws of the Agathyrsi, a nation in Sarmatia, were all delivered in verse. Not to mention the known laws of the Twelve Tables, which, from the fragments still remaining of them, appear to have consisted of short rythmic sentences.

From laws and religion poetry made an easy progress to the celebration of the Gods and Heroes, who were their founders. Verses in their praise were sung on solemn occasions by the composers, or bards themselves. We meet with many before Homer, who distinguished themselves by such productions. Fabricius † has enumerated near seventy whose names have reached our times. That immortal author had the advantage of

* Jamblichus de vita Pythag. *passim*; and particularly *lib.* I. cap. 15. & 25.

† In Bibliotheca Græca, *tom.* I.

hearing their poems repeated; and was certainly in-
debted to his predecessors for many beauties which we
admire as original. That he was himself an ΑΟΙΔΟΣ,
or Minstrel, and sung his own verses to the lyre, is
shown by the admirable author of the Enquiry into his
Life and Writings *. Nor were his poems rescued from
the uncertain fame of tradition, and committed to wri-
ting till some time after his death †.

Such was the utility of the poetic tradition among
the more polished nations of antiquity: and with those
they denominated Barbarians we find it no less practised ‡.
The Persians had their Magi, who preserved, as would
seem in this way, the remarkable events of former times;
and in war went before the army singing the praises of
their illustrious men, whom the extraordinary gratitude
and admiration of their countrymen had exalted into
Deities. If they gained the victory, the Song of Triumph
recorded the deeds of those who had fallen, and by their
praises animated the ambition of those who enjoyed the
conquest to further acts of valour. The latter custom

---

* Sect. VIII.

† Ælian. Var. Hist. lib. xiii. c. 14.

‡ The reader, who would desire more intelligence on this head, may consult a curious *Dissertation on the Monuments which supplied the Defect of Writing among the first Historians*, by the Abbé Anselm, in Les Memoires de l'Academie des Inscriptions, &c.

was

was in use still more anciently among the Jews, as appears from the beautiful songs of Moses * and Deborah †
preserved in Sacred Writ.

The Druids of Gaul and Britain afford a noted instance ‡. Such firm hold did their traditions take of the memory that some of them are retained in the minds of their countrymen to this very day §. The

* Exod. XV.   † Judges V.

‡ Et Bardi quidem fortia virorum illustrium facta heroicis compositâ versibus, cum dulcibus lyrae modulis cantitarunt. *Ammian. Marcell.* lib. xvi.

§ Atque horum (Bardorum seu Druidarum) cantiones, aut ad similitudinem potius earundem fictae etiamnum aliquae extant *die Meister Gesänge*, sed recentiores pleraeque, nec vel quingentos annos excedentes. *Beſſel. in notis ad Eginhart.* Traject. 1711, *p.* 130. Nonnulli eruditi viri observarunt veterem illam Gallorum consuetudinem *(scil.* visci sacrum usum apud druidas) etiam nunc multis Galliae locis retineri, cum anni initio clamitant, *Au guy l'an neuf.* i. e. Ad viscum; annus novus. *Hotoman. ad Caeſ. l.* 6. Druydes vero Heduorum, qui tunc habitabant in quodam loco, hodiernis temporibus Mons druidum dictus, distans a nostra civitate Heduensi per unum milliare ubi adhuc restant vestigia loci habitationis eorum, utebantur pro eorum armis anguibus in campo azureo; habebant etiam in parte superiore ramum visci quercinei *(ung rameaul de guyg de chasne)* et in parte inferiore unum cumulum parvorum anguium seu serpentium argenteorum quasi tunc nascentium, qui vulgo dicitur, *coubee de serpens d'argent*. *Chaſſeneuz* Catalogi Gloriae mundi, 1529, *folio verso* 26.

Germans,

Germans, as we learn from Tacitus, had no other mode of commemorating the transactions of past times than by verse. The brave actions of their ancestors were always sung as an incentive to their imitation before they entered into combat. The like we read of the ancient Goths *, those destroyers of all literature, who yet possessed greater skill in the fine arts than is commonly ascribed to them. From them this custom passed to their descendants the inhabitants of the Northern regions; many animated specimens of whose traditional poetry have been preserved to our times † and quoted by their modern historians as uncontroulable vouchers. As the Arabian historians refer for the truth of many events to the Spanish romanzes, saved in like manner by tradition for many ages; many of which are of very remote antiquity, and abound with the higher beauties of poetry ‡. Traditional verses are to this day a favourite amusement of the Mahometan nations, Though, instead of recording the illustrious actions of their real heroes, they chaunt the fabled exploits of

* Jornand. See *Warton's Hist. of English Poetry.*

† See the Histories of Saxo Grammat. Jo. Magnus, Torfæus, &c. *passim*; and Dr. Percy's *Five Pieces of Runic Poetry.*

‡ *Hist. de las guerras civiles de Granada.* A most beautiful imitation of their manner may be found among the Poems of Voiture. The Spanish word *Romanze* seems now applied to any short lyric tale on whatever subject. We find in Gongora, their most eminent poet, *Romances Amorosos, y Burlescos.*

Buhalul

Buhalul their Orlando *, or the yet more ridiculous ones of their Prophet †. From them it would appear that rime, that great help to the remembrance of traditional poetry, paſſed to the Troubadours of Provence; who from them ſeem alſo to have received the ſpirit and character of their effuſions. Like them they compoſed amorous verſes with delicacy and nature; but when they attemptted the ſublimer walk of the Heroic Song, their imagination was often bewildered, and they wandered into the contiguous regions of the incredible and abſurd ‡.

In proportion as Literature advanced in the world Oral Tradition diſappeared. The venerable Britiſh Bards were in time ſucceeded by the Welſh Beirdh §,

* Huet, Lettre à Monſieur Segrais, ſnr l'origine des Romans, p. LXVII. edit. d'Amſt. 1715.

† Hiſtoriale deſcription de l'Afrique, eſcrite de notre temps par Jean Leon, African, premierement en langue Arabeſque, puis en Toſcane, et à preſent miſe en François—En Anvers, 1556. *lib.* III. *p.* 175.

A curious ſpecimen of the Eaſtern religious poetry may be ſeen in Sir John Chardin's Voyage to Perſia, vol. I.

‡ Huet, ubi ſupra, p. LXX. Ermengarde vicomteſſe de Narbonne——L'accueil favorable qu'elle fit aux Poetes Provençeaux, a fait croire qu'elle tenoit cour *d'amour* dans ſon Palais, mourut 1194. Almanach Hiſtorique de Languedoc, A Touloufe, 1752, p. 277. See Hiſt. Liter. des Troub. *Paris,* 1774. Tranſlations of Provenzal Sirventes, and an imitation of the Provenzal Heroic Romanze, may be found in a volume lately publiſhed by Mr. Dilly, intituled, RIMES. Odes, Book II. Odes, 8, 9, 10, 11, 12, 13. 16.

§ Hiſtory of Wales by Caradoc of Lhancarvan, &c. 1702. p. 159.

whoſe

whose principal occupation seems to have been to preserve the genealogy of their patrons, or at times to amuse them with some fabulous story of their predecessors sung to the harp or crowd *, an instrument which Griffith ap Conan, King of Wales, is said to have brought from Ireland, about the beginning of the twelfth century.

In like manner, among the Caledonians, as an ingenious writer † acquaints us, "Every chief in process "of time had a bard in his family, and the office be- "came hereditary. By the succession of these bards the "poems concerning the ancestors of the family were "handed down from generation to generation; they "were repeated to the whole clan on solemn occasions, "and always alluded to in the new compositions of the "bards." The successors of Ossian the first of poets were at length employed chiefly in the mean office of preserving fabulous genealogies, and flattering the pride of their chieftains at the expence of truth, without

* This is the instrument meant in the following verses of Ven. Fortunatus, lib. vii.

Romanusque lyra plaudat tibi, barbarus harpa,
 Græcus Achilliaca, Crotta Britanna canat.

See more of the Harp in War. Antiq. Hibern. cap. 22. And Mr. Evans, Dissert. de Bardis, p. 80.

† Mr. Macpherson, in his Dissertation on the Era of Ossian, p. 228. ed. 1773.

even

even fancy sufficient to render their inventions either pleasing or plausible. That order of men, I believe, is now altogether extinct; yet they have left a spirit of poetry in the country where they flourished*; and Ossian's harp still yields a dying sound among the wilds of Morven.

Having thus given a faint view of the progress of the Oral Tradition of Poetry to these times, I proceed to shew what arts the ancient bards employed to make their verses take such hold of the memory of their countrymen, as to be transmitted safe and entire without the aid of writing for many ages. These may be considered as affecting the passions and the ear. Their mode of expression was simple and genuine. They of consequence touched the passions truly and effectively. And when the passions are engaged, we listen with avidity to the tale that so agreeably affects them; and remember it again with the most prompt facility. This may be observed in children, who will forget no circumstance of an interesting story, more especially if striking or dreadful to the fancy; when they cannot remember a short maxim which only occupies the judgement. The passions of men have been and will be the same through all ages. Poetry is the sovereign of the passions, and will reign while they

* See Martin's, and other Descriptions of the Western Isles, passim.

exist. We may laugh at Sir Isaac Newton, as we have at Descartes; but we shall always admire a Homer, an Ossian, or a Shakspeare.

As the subjects of these genuine painters of nature deeply interested the heart, and by that means were so agreeable and affecting, that every hearer wished to remember them; so their mode of constructing their verse was such, that the remembrance was easy and expeditious. A few of their many arts to aid the memory I shall here enumerate.

I. Most of these Oral poems were set to music, as would appear, by the original authors themselves. That this was the custom so early as the days of Homer, may be seen in the excellent author formerly adduced *. How should we have been affected by hearing a composition of Homer or Ossian, sung and played by these immortal masters themselves! With the poem the air seems to have passed from one age to another; but as no musical compositions of the Greeks exist, we are quite in the dark as to the nature of these. I suppose that Ossian's poetry is still recited to its original cadence and to appropriated tunes. We find, in an excellent modern writer †, that this mode of singing poetry to the harp was reckoned an accomplishment so late as among the Saxon Ecclesiastics. The ancient

* Enquiry, &c. Sect. 8.
† Mr. Warton in his History of English Poetry.

music was confessedly infinitely superior to ours in the command of the passions. Nay, the music of the most barbarous countries has had effects that not all the sublime pathos of Corelli, or animated strains of Handel, could produce. Have not the Welsh, Irish, and Scottish tunes, greater influence over the most informed mind at this day than the best Italian concerto? What modern refined music could have the powers of the *Rance de Vaches* * of the Swifs, or the melancholy found of the Indian Bansha †? Is not the war-music of the rudest inhabitants of the wilds of America or Scotland more terrible to the ear than that of the best band in the British army? Or what is still more surprizing, will not the softer passions be more inflamed by a

---

* See Rousseau, Dict. de Musique, *sur cette article*. Though the Swifs are a brave nation, yet their dance, which corresponds to the *Rance des Vaches*, is like their others, rather expressive of an effeminate spirit. ' Les dances des Suisses consistent en un continuel
' trainement de Jambe, ces pas repondoient mal au courage ferme de
' cette nation. Coquillart en son Blazon des armes, et des dames.'

> ' Les Escossoys font les repliques,
> ' Pragois et Bretons bretonnans,
> ' Les Suisses dancent leurs Moresques,
> ' A touts leurs tabourins sonnans.'
> Monf. L. D. Notes à Rabelais, Tom. IV. p. 164. 1725.

† See Grainger's Proso-poetic Account of the Culture of the Sugar-cane, Book IV.

Turkish air than by the most exquisite effort of a polite composer? As we learn from an elegant author [*], whom concurring circumstances rendered the best judge that could be imagined of that subject. The harmony therefore of the old traditional songs possessing such influence over the passions, at the same time that it rendered every expression necessary to the ear, must have greatly recommended them to the remembrance.

II. Besides musical cadence, many arts were used in the versification to facilitate the rehearsal. Such were:

1. The frequent returns of the same sentences and descriptions expressed in the very same words. As for instance, the delivery of messages, the description of battles, &c. Of which we meet with infinite examples in Homer, and some, if I mistake not, in Ossian. Good ones may be found in Hardyknute, Part I. v. 123. &c. compared with Part II. v. 167, &c. and in Child Maurice, v. 31, with v. 67; and innumerable such in the ancient Traditional Poetry of all nations. These served as land-marks, in the view of which the memory travelled secure over the intervening spaces. On this head falls likewise to be mentioned, what we call The Burden, that is, the unvaried repetition of one or more lines fixing the tone of the poem throughout the whole. That this is very ancient among the barbaric nations, may be gathered from the known Song of Regner Lodbrog,

---

[*] Letters of Lady M. W. Montague, XXXIII.

Lodbrog, to be found in Olaus Wormius *; every stanza of which begins with one and the same line. So many of our ballads, both ancient and modern, have this aid to the memory, that it is unnecessary to condescend on any in particular.

2. Alliteration was before the invention of rime greatly used, chiefly by the nations of Northern original to affist the remembrance of their traditional poetry. Most of the Runic methods of versification consisted in this practice. It was the only one among the Saxon poets, from whom it passed to the English and Scottish †. When rime became common, this which

was

---

* Regner Lodbrog, King of Denmark, flourished in the Ninth Century.

† See Hickes, *Ling. Vet. Sept. Thes. c.* 23. From the Saxons he observes, that the author of *Pierce Plowman* drew this practice, c. 21. This poem was written about 1350. There is a remarkable similarity in its style and manner with those very curious pieces of ancient Scottish poetry, stiled The Prophecies of Thomas Rymer, Marvellous Merling, Beid, Berlington, Waldhave, Eltrainc, Banister, and Sybilla, printed at Edinburgh in 1615, and reprinted from that edition, 1741, 8vo. It is very surprising that the respectable editor of *Ancient Scottish Poems, from the MS. of George Bannatyne*, 1568. *Edin.* 1770, seems to regard these as no ancienter than the time of Queen Mary. His reasons are only founded on the modern appearance of some particular passages. That they have been modernized and corrupted, I will readily allow;

was before thought to constitute the sole difference betwixt prose and verse, was still regarded as an accessary

allow; but that they are on the main nearly as ancient as Rymer's time, who died about the beginning of the 14th Century, I believe the learned must confess from intrinsic evidence, in such cases the surest of all. Not to mention that Sir David Lindsay, who wrote in the reign of James V. is an undoubted witness that they must be more ancient than this eminent Antiquary would infer. For in enumerating the methods he took to divert that prince while under his care in his infancy, after condescending on some risible circumstances, as

> Whan thou wast young I bare thee in my arm
> Full tenderly till thou began to gang;
> And in thy bed oft happed thee full warm,
> With lute in hand then sweetly to thee sang,
> Sometime in dancing fiercefully I flang,
> And sometimes playing farses on the flure,
> And sometimes of mine office taking cure.
>
> And sometimes like a feind transfigurate,
> And sometime like a greesy ghost of gay,
> In divers forms of times disfigurate, &c.

He adds,

> The Prophesies of *Rymer*, *Bede*, and *Merlin*,
> And many other pleasant history
> Of the red *Etin*, and *Gyre Carlin*,
> Comforting thee when that I saw thee sory.

Epistle to the King, prefixed to his Dream.

fary grace, and was carried to a ludicrous length by some poets of no mean rank in both nations. So late

They begin thus:

> Merling fays in his book, who will read right,
> Althouch his fayings be uncouth, they fhall be true found,
> In the feventh chapter read who fo will,
> One thoufand and more after Chrift's birth.
> Then the Chalnalider of Cornwall is called,
> And the wolf out of Wales is vanquifhed for aye,
> Then many ferlies fhall fall, and many folk fhall die.

This exordium is evidently retouched by a modern hand.—But very many of the paffages feem to ftand in their original form, as the following lines, which are all in the Saxon manner, will teftify:

> And derfly dung down without any doome—
> A proud prince in the preis lordly fhall light,
> With bold Barons in bufhment to battle fhall wend.——
> There fhall a galyart goat with a golden horn.———

And many fimilar. That prophecy which bears the name of Thomas Rymer is not deftitute of poetic graces. It opens with the following lines:

> Still on my ways as I went
> Out throuch a land befide a lee,
> I met a bairn upon the bent *,
> Methought him feemly for to fee,

* *Modernized way, though againft the rime.*

I afked

late as the reign of Queen Elizabeth we find the following lines in a court poet:

> Princes puff'd; barons blustered; lords began lowr,
> Knights storm'd; squires startled, like steeds in a stowr;
> Pages and yeomen yelled out in the hall *.

And William Dunbar, the chief of the old Scottish poets, begins a copy of verses to the King thus,
Sanct Salvator send silver sorrow †.

> I asked him wholly his intent;
> Good Sir, if your will be,
> Since that ye bide upon the bent,
> Some uncouth tidings tell you me:
> When shall all these wars be gone?
> That leil men may live in lee;
> Or when shall Falsehude go from home,
> And Lawtie blow his horn on hie?
> I looked from me not a mile,
> And saw twa knights upon a lee, &c.

I imagine, however, they are all the composures of one hand; and, if I may use a conjecture, were written immediately after the visions of Pierce Plowman, every English poem of note in those days being soon succeeded by an imitation in Scotland.

* *King Ryence's Challenge,* in the Reliques of Ancient English Poetry. *Vol.* III. p. 27.

† Bannatyne's Scottish Poems, p. 68.

III. But the greatest assistance that could be found to the tradition of poetry was derived from the invention of rime; which is far more ancient than is commonly believed. One of the most learned men this age has produced *, has shewn that it is common in Scripture. All the Psalms consist of riming verses, and many other passages which he names. They were used among the Greeks so early as the time of Gorgias the Sicilian, who taught the Athenians this practice. And though the spirit of the Greek and Latin languages did not always admit of them in poetry, yet they were used as occasional beauties by their most celebrated writers. Homer, Hesiod, and Virgil, have a few, though apparently more from chance than design. The ancient Saturnine verses were all rimes, as an old commentator † informs us. And it is more than probable they were so constructed merely that the memory might the more easily preserve them, their licence forbidding their being committed to writing. Those who would wish to know more particularly the universality of this mode of versifying among the other ancient nations, may consult the *Huetiana* of the most learned and respectable Bishop of Avranches ‡. The Eastern poetry consists altogether, if I mistake not, of riming lines, as may be observed in the specimens of Hafiz their most

* Le Clerc, Biblioth. Universelle, tom. IX.
† Servius ad Georg. II. ver. 386.
‡ Sect. 78.

illustrious

illustrious writer, lately published *. It appears, however, that alliteration supplied the place of rime with the Northern nations till within a recent period †. Ossian's poetry, I suppose, is in stanzas something like our ballad measure; though it were to be wished the translator had favoured us with some information on this head evidenced by large specimens of the original. He indeed acquaints us that "Each verse was so connected with those which preceded, or followed it, that if one line had been remembered in a stanza, it was almost impossible to forget the rest ‡:" but this stands greatly in need of explanation.

The common ballad stanza is so simple, that it has been used by most nations as the first mode of constructing rimes. The Spanish romanzes bear a great resemblance in this, as in other respects, to the Scottish Ballads. In both, every alternate line ends with similar vowels, though the consonants are not so strictly attended to. As for instance, in the former we have *bana, espada; mala, palabra; vega, cueva; rompan, volcanos;* for rimes: and in the later, *middle, girdle; keep, bleed; Buleighan, tak him;* &c. The English, even in the ruder pieces of their first minstrels, seem to have

* Jones, Comment. Poeseos Asiaticæ—Richardson's Specimen of Persian Poetry.
† Ol. Worm. Lit. Run. p. 165 & 176.
‡ Dissert. on the Era of Ossian, p. 228. ed. 1773.

paid

paid more attention to the correspondence of their consonants, as may be observed in the curious Collection published by Dr. Percy.

As the simplicity of this stanza rendered it easy to the composer, and likewise more natural to express the passions, so it added to the facility of recollection. It's tone is sedate and slow. The rimes occur seldom, and at equal distances: though when a more violent passion is to be painted, by doubling the rimes, they at once expressed the mind better, and diversified the harmony. Of this the reader will observe many instances in this collection, as, *Here maun I lie, here maun I die: Like beacon bricht at deid of nicht: Na river heir, my dame sa deir:* &c. and, to give a very solemn movement to the cadence, they sometimes tripled the rime, an instance of which may be observed in the first stanza of Child Maurice.

When all the circumstances here hinted at are considered, we shall be less apt to wonder, that, by the concurrence of musical air, retentive arts in the composition, and chiefly of rime, the most noble productions of former periods have been preserved in the memory of a succession of admirers, and have had the good fortune to arrive at our times pure and uncorrupted.

DISSERTATION II.

ON THE TRAGIC BALLAD.

THAT species of poetry which we denominate Ballad, is peculiar to a barbarous period. In an advanced state of arts, the Comic Ballad assumes the form of the Song or Sonnet, and the Tragic or Heroic Ballad that of the higher Ode.

The cause of our pleasure in seeing a mournful event represented, or hearing it described, has been attempted to be explained by many critics*. It seems to arise from the mingled passions of Admiration of the art of the author, Curiosity to attend the termination, Delight arising from a reflection on our own security, and the Sympathetic Spirit.

---

* Aristotle, Scaliger, Dubos, Trapp in his Prælections, Hume, Essay on Tragedy; but above all Mr. Burke in his Enquiry into the Sublime and Beautiful.

In giving this pleasure, perhaps the Tragic Ballad yields to no effort of human genius. When we peruse a polished Tragedy or Ode, we admire the art of the author, and are led to praise the invention; but when we read an unartful description of a melancholy event, our passions are more intensely moved. The laboured productions of the informed composer resemble a Greek or Roman temple; when we enter it, we admire the art of the builder. The rude effusions of the Gothic Muse are like the monuments of their Architecture. We are filled with a religious reverence, and, forgetting our praise of the contriver, adore the present deity.

I believe no Tragic Ballad of renowned Antiquity has reached our times, if we deny the beautiful and pathetic CARMEN DE ATY in Catullus a title to this class; which, as a modern critic of note has observed*, seems a translation from some Greek *Dithyrambic* †, far more ancient than the times of that poet. His translation of Sappho's Ode might shew that he took a delight in the ancient Greek compositions, from which indeed he seems to have derived in a great measure his peculiarly delicate vein.

* Essay on the writings and genius of Pope, *p.* 324. 3*d ed.*

† The *Dithyrambics* were Heroic Songs, written with the highest glow of poetic fancy in honour of the ancient deities. Aristotle informs us, that the Greek Tragedy originated from them; as their Comedy did from their Pastoral Love Songs.

But

But it was with the nations in a state of barbarity, that this effusion of the heart flourished as in it's proper soil; their societies, rude and irregular, were full of vicissitudes, and every hour subject to the most dreadful accidents. The Minstrels, who only knew, and were inspired by the present manners, caught the tale of mortality, and recorded it for the instruction and entertainment of others. It pleased by moving the passions, and, at the same time, afforded caution to their auditors to guard against similar mis-adventures.

It is amusing to observe how expressive the poetry of every country is of its real manners. That of the Northern nations is ferocious to the highest degree Nor need we wonder that those, whose laws obliged them to decide the most trifling debate with the sword*, delighted in a vein of poetry, which only painted deeds of blood, and objects horrible to the imagination. The ballad poetry of the Spaniards is tinged with the romantic gallantry of that nation. The hero is all complaisance; and takes off his helmet in the heat of combat, when he thinks on his mistress. That of the English is generous and brave. In their most noble ballad, Percy laments over the death of his

---

* Frotho etiam III. Danorum rex, quemadmodum Saxo, lib. V. refert, de qualibet controversia ferro decerni sanxit; speciosius viribus quam verbis, confligendum existimans. *Schedius de diis Ger. Syng.* II. c. 46.

mortal

mortal foe. That of the Scots is perhaps, like the face of their country, more various than the rest. We find in it the bravery of the English, the gallantry of the Spanish, and I am afraid in some instances the ferocity of the Northern.

A late writer * has remarked, that, " the Scottish " tunes, whether melancholy or gay; whether amorous, " martial, or pastoral, are in a style highly original, " and most feelingly expressive of all the passions from " the sweetest to the most terrible." He proceeds, " Who was it that thew out those dreadful wild ex- " pressions of distraction and melancholy in *Lady Cul-* " *rofs's Dream?* an old composition, now I am afraid " lost, perhaps because it was almost too terrible for " the ear."

This composition is neither lost, nor is it too terrible for the ear. On the contrary, a child might hear it repeated in a winter night without the smallest emotion. A copy † of it now lyes before me, and as some

---

* Miscellanies by John Armstrong, M. D. vol. II. p. 254.

† It is intituled, " A Godly Dream compiled by Elizabeth " Melvil, Lady Culross younger, at the request of a freind." Edinburgh, 1737, 12mo. p. 20. It is either reprinted from some former edition, or from a MS. It was written, I conjecture, about the end of the Sixteenth Century; but in this edition I suspect several expressions are modernized and altered to accommodate it to the common capacity.

curiosity

curiosity may have been raised by the above remark, I shall here give an account of it. The dreadful and melancholy of this production are solely of the religious kind, and may have been deeply affecting to the enthusiastic at the period in which it was wrote: It begins thus;

> Upon a day as I did mourn full sore,
> For sundry things wherewith my soul was grieved,
> My grief increased, and grew more and more,
> I comfort fled, and could not be relieved;
> With heaviness my heart was sore mischieved,
> I loathed my life, I could not eat nor drink,
> I might not speak, nor look to none that lived,
> But mused alone, and diverse things did think.
>
> This wretched world did so molest my mind,
> I thought upon this false and iron age,
> And how our hearts are so to vice inclined,
> That Satan seems most fearfully to rage,
> Nothing on earth my sorrow could aswage,
> I felt my sin so strongly to increase;
> I grieved the spirit was wont to be my pledge;
> My soul was plunged into most deep distress.

Her Saviour is then supposed to appear in a dream, and lead her through many hair-breadth scapes into Heaven:

Through dreadful dens, which made my heart aghast,
He bare me up when I began to tire;
Sometimes we clamb oer cragie mountains high;
And sometimes stayed on ugly braes of sand,
They were so stay that wonder was to see;
But when I feared, he held me by the hand.—
Through great deserts we wandered on our way.—
Forward we past on narrow bridge of tree,
Oer waters great which hideously did roar, &c.

The most terrible passage to a superstitious ear, is that in which she supposes herself suspended over the Gulph of Perdition:

Ere I was ware, one gripped me at last,
And held me high above a flaming fire.
The fire was great, the heat did pierce me sore,
My faith grew weak, my grip was very small.
I trembled fast, my fear grew more and more.
My hands did shake that I held him withall,
At length they loosed, then I began to fall, &c.

At length she arrives in view of the Heavenly mansions in a stanza, which, to alter a little her own expression, 'Glisters with *tinsel*.'

I looked up unto that castle fair
Glistering with gold; and shining silver bright
The stately towers did mount above the air;
They blinded me they cast so great a light,
My heart was glad to see that joyful sight,
My voyage then I thought it not in vain,
I him besought to guide me there aright,
With many vows never to tire again.

And the whole concludes with an exhortation to a pious life.

But what has the Christian religion to do with poetry? In the true poetic terrible, I believe, some passages in Hardyknute yield to no attempt of a strong and dark fancy. The Ballad styled Edward may, I fear, be rather adduced as an evidence that this displeases, when it rises to a degree of the horrible, which that singular piece certainly partakes of.

The Pathetic is the other principal walk of the Tragic Muse: and in this the Scottish Ballads yield to no compositions whatever. What can be imagined more moving than the catastrophes of Ossian's Darthula, the most pathetic of all poems? or of Hardyknute,

nute, Child Maurice, and indeed moſt of the pieces now collected? Were ever the feelings of a fond mother expreſſed in language equal in ſimplicity and pathos to that of Lady Bothwell?—This leads me to remark, that the dialect in which the Scottiſh Ballads are written gives them a great advantage in point of touching the paſſions. Their language is rough and unpoliſhed, and ſeems to flow immediately from the heart *. We meet with no concettos or far-fetched thoughts in them. They poſſeſs the pathetic power in the higheſt degree, becauſe they do not affect it; and are ſtriking, becauſe they do not meditate to ſtrike.

Moſt of the compoſitions now offered to the publick, have already received approbation. The mutilated Fragment of Hardyknute formerly in print, was admired and celebrated by the best critics. As it is now, I am inclined to think, given in it's original perfection, it is certainly the moſt noble production in this ſtyle that ever appeared in the world. The manners and characters are ſtrongly marked, and well preſerved. The incidents deeply intereſting; and the cataſtrophe new and affecting. I am indebted for moſt of the ſtanzas, now recovered, to the memory of a lady in Lanarkſhire.

* Ὁ γὰρ ὄγκος δὲ τὸ ἐξ ἐπιτηδεύσεω; ἅπαν ἀνθοποίητον.
Dionyſ. Hal.

A modern lyric poet of the first class* has pronounced Child Maurice a Divine Ballad. "Aristotle's "best rules," says he, "are observed in it in a manner that shews the author had never read Aristotle." Indeed, if any one will peruse Aristotle's Art of Poetry with Dacier's Elucidations, and afterwards compare their most approved rules with this simple Ballad, he will find that they are better illustrated by this rude effort of the Gothic Muse, than by the most exquisite Tragedy of ancient or modern times. The Œdipus Tyrannus of Sophocles, the Athalie of Racine, the Merope of Maffei, and even the very excellent Drama, which seems immediately founded on it, not excepted. There being many delicate strokes in this original, which the plot adopted by that author forbad his making proper use of. This does honour at once to the unknown composer of this Ballad, and to the first of critics. In the former the reader will admire a genius, that, probably untracked by erudition, could produce a story corresponding to the intricate though natural rules of the Greek author. To the latter will be readily confirmed the applause of an ancient †, that, he was the secretary of Nature, and his pen was ever dipped in good sense.

* Mr. Gray. See his Letters published by Mr. Mason. Sect. IV. Let. XXV.

† Apud Suidam.

These,

Thefe, and the other monuments of ancient Scottifh Poetry, which have already appeared, are in this edition given much more correct; and a few are now firft publifhed from tradition. The Editor imagined they poffeffed fome fmall beauties, elfe they would not have been added to this Selection. Their feeming antiquity was only regarded as it enhanced their real graces.

MDCCLXXVI *.

* Thefe Differtations, &c. were written of this date, but flight additions have been made to them from time to time; as the reader will obferve from references to books publifhed fince that period.

> LA PLUPART DE CES CHANSONS SONT DE VIEILLES RO-
> MANCES DONT LES AIRS NE SONT PAS PIQUANS; MAIS ILS
> ONT JE NE SAIS QUOI D'ANTIQUE ET DE DOUX QUI TOUCHE
> A LA LONGUE.
> ROUSSEAU.

HARDYKNUTE.

AN HEROIC BALLAD.

PART I.

STATELY stept he east the ha,
    And stately stept he west;
Full seventy yeirs he now had sene,
    With scerce sevin yeirs of rest.
He livit whan Britons breach of faith   5
    Wrocht Scotland meikle wae,
And ay his sword tauld to their cost
    He was their deidly fae.

Hie on a hill his castle stude,
    With halls and touris a hicht,   10
And gudely chambers fair to see,
    Whar he lodgit mony a knicht.
His dame sa peirles anes, and fair,
    For chaste, and bewtie, sene,
Na marrow had in a the land,   15
    Save Emergard the quene.

Full thirtein fons to him fhe bare,
　　All men of valour ftout,
In bluidy ficht, with fword in hand,
　　Nyne loft their lives bot doubt;　　　20
Four yit remaind; lang mote they live
　　To ftand by liege and land:
Hie was their fame, hie was their micht,
　　And hie was their command.

Greit luve they bare to Fairly fair,　　25
　　Their fifter faft and deir,
Her girdle fhawd her middle jimp,
　　And gowden glift her hair.
What waefou wae her bewtie bred!
　　Waefou to young and auld,　　　　30
Waefou I trow to kyth and kin,
　　As ftory ever tauld.

The King of Norfe, in fummer tide,
　　Puft up with pouir and micht,
Landed in fair Scotland the yle,　　　35
　　Wi mony a hardie knicht.
The tidings to our gude Scots king
　　Came as he fat at dyne
With noble chiefs in braive aray,
　　Drinking the bluid red wyne.　　　40

　　　　　　　　　　　　　　"To

" To horſe, to horſe, my royal liege!
" Your faes ſtand on the ſtrand;
" Full twenty thouſand glittering ſpeirs
" The cheifs of Norſe command.
" Bring me my ſteid Mage dapple gray."   45
Our gude king raiſe and cryd:
A truſtier beiſt in all the land,
  A Scots king nevir ſeyd.

" Gae, little page, tell Hardyknute,
" Wha lives on hill ſa hie,   50
" To draw his ſword, the dreid of faes,
" And haſte and follow me."
The little page flew ſwift as dart,
  Flung by his maſter's arm;
' Cum down, cum down, lord Hardyknute,   55
' And red your king frae harm.'

Then reid, reid grew his dark-brown cheiks
  Sae did his dark-brown brow;
His luiks grew kene, as they were wont
  In danger grit to do.   60
He has tane a horn as grene as graſs,
  And gien five ſounds ſa ſhrill,
That tries in grene wode ſhuke thereat,
  Sae loud rang ilka hill.

His sons in manly sport and glie 65
 Had past the summer's morn;
Whan lo! down in a grassy dale,
 They heard their father's horn.
' That horn, quoth they, neir sounds in peace,
 ' We have other sport to bide;' 70
And sune they hied them up the hill,
 And sune were at his side.

"Late, late yestrene, I weind in peace
 " To end my lengthend lyfe;
" My age micht well excuse my arm 75
 " Frae manly feats of stryfe:
" But now that Norse does proudly boast
 " Fair Scotland to enthral,
" It's neir be said of Hardyknute,
 " He feird to fecht or fall. 80

" Robin of Rothsay bend thy bow,
 " Thy arrows shute sa leil,
" That mony a comely countenance
 " They've turn'd to deidly pale.
" Braive Thomas take ye but your lance, 85
 " Ye neid na weapons mair;
" Gif ye fecht wi't, as ye did anes,
 " Gainst Westmoreland's ferce heir.

         " And

" And Malcolm, licht of fute as ftag
    " That runs in foreft wilde,   90
" Get me my thoufands thrie of men
    " Weil bred to fword and fhield:
" Bring me my horfe and harnifine,
    " My blade of metal clere."
If faes but kend the hand it bare,   95
    They fune had fled for feir.

" Fareweil my dame fae peirlefs gude,"
    And tuke her by the hand,
" Fairer to me in age you feim
    " Than maids for bewtie famd: 100
" My youngeft fon fall here remain,
    " To guard thefe ftately touirs,
" And fhute the filver bolt that keips
    " Sae faft your painted bowers."

And firft fhe wet her comly cheiks,   105
    And then her boddice grene;
The filken cords of twirtle twift
    Were plet with filver fhene;
And apron fet with mony a dye
    Of neidle-wark fae rare,   110
Wove by nae hand, as ye may guefs,
    Save that of Fairly fair.

And he has ridden our muir and mofs,
   Our hills and mony a glen,
Whan he cam to a wounded knicht,   115
   Making a heavy mane:
' Here maun I lye, here maun I dye
   ' By treacheries faufe gyles;
' Witlefs I was that eir gave faith
   ' To wicked woman's fmyles.'   120

" Sir knicht, gin ye were in my bouir,
   " To lean on filken feat,
" My lady's kyndlie care you'd pruve
   " Wha neir kend deidly hate;
" Hirfell wald watch ye all the day,   125
   " Hir maids at deid of nicht;
" And Fairly fair your heart would cheir,
   " As fhe ftands in your ficht.

" Arife, young knicht, and mount your fteid,
   " Bricht lows the fhynand day;   130
" Chufe frae my menie wham ye pleife,
   " To leid ye on the way."
Wi fmylefs luik, and vifage wan
   The wounded knicht replyd,
' Kynd chieftain your intent purfue,   135
   ' For heir I maun abide.

          ' To

' To me nae after day nor nicht
   ' Can eir be sweit or fair;
' But sune benethe sum draping trie,
   ' Cauld dethe sall end my care.'   140
Still him to win strave **Hardyknute**,
   Nor strave he lang in vain;
Short pleiding eithly micht prevale,
   Him to his lure to gain.

" I will return wi speid to bide,   145
   " Your plaint and mend your wae:
" But private grudge maun neir be quelled,
   " Before our countries fae.
" Mordac, thy eild may best be spaird
   " The fields of stryfe fraemang;   150
" Convey Sir knicht to my abode,
   " And meise his egre pang."

Syne he has gane far hynd, out owr
   Lord **Chattan's** land sae wyde;
That lord a worthy wicht was ay,   155
   Whan faes his courage seyd:
Of Pictish race, by mother's side;
   Whan Picts ruled Caledon,
Lord **Chattan** claimd the princely maid,
   When he savd Pictish crown.   160

Now with his ferce and ftalwart train
  He recht a rifing hicht,
Whar braid encampit on the dale,
  Norfe army lay in ficht;
" Yonder my valiant fons, full ferce   165
  " Our raging rievers wait,
" On the unconquerit Scottifh fwaird
  " To try with us their fate.

" Mak orifons to him that fav'd
  " Our fauls upon the rude;   170
" Syne braively fhaw your veins are filld
  " Wi Caledonian bluid."
Then furth he drew his truftie glaive,
  While thoufands all around,
Drawn frae their fheiths glanc'd in the fun, 175
  And loud the bugils found.

To join his king, adown the hill
  In hafte his march he made,
While playand pibrochs minftrals meit
  Afore him ftately ftrade.   180
' Thrife welcum, valiant ftoup of weir,
  ' Thy nation's fheild and pride,
' Thy king na reafoun has to feir,
  ' Whan thou art by his fide.

Whan bows were bent, and darts were thrawn, 185
  For thrang fcerce cold they flie,
The darts clave arrows as they met,
  Eir faes their dint mote drie.
Lang did they rage, and fecht full ferce,
  Wi little fkaith to man; 190
But bluidy, bluidy was the feild
  Or that lang day was done!

The king of Scots that findle bruik'd
  The war that luik'd like play,
Drew his braid fword, and brake his bow, 195
  Sen bows feim'd but delay.
Quoth noble Rothfay, ' Mine I'll keep,
  ' I wate it's bleid a fcore.'
" Hafte up my merrie men," cryd the king,
  As he rade on before. 200

The king of Norfe he focht to find,
  Wi him to menfe the faucht;
But on his forehead there did licht
  A fharp unfonfie fhaft:
As he his hand pat up to feil 205
  The wound, an arrow kein,
O waefu chance! there pind his hand
  In midft atweene his eyne.

' Revenge!

'Revenge! revenge!' cryd Rothſay's heir,
  'Your mail-coat ſall nocht bide
'The ſtrenth and ſharpneſs of my dart,'
  Whilk ſnared the riever's ſide.
Anither arrow weil he mark'd
  It perc'd his neck in twa;
His hands then quat the ſilver reins,
  He law as eard did fa.

'Sair bleids my liege! Sair, ſair he bleids!'
  Again with micht he drew,
And geſture dreid his ſturdy bow;
  Faſt the braid arrow flew:
Wae to the knicht he ettled at;
  Lament now quene Elgreid;
Hire dames to wail your darling's fall,
  His youth, and comely meid.

'Tak aff, tak aff his coſtly jupe,'
  (Of gold well was it twynd,
Knit like the fowlers net, throuch whilk
  His ſteily harnes ſhynd.)
'Beir Norie that gift frae me, and bid
  'Him venge the bluid it weirs;
'Say if he face my bended bow
  'He ſure na weapon ſeirs.'

Proud Norſe with giant body tall,
  Braid ſhoulder, and arms ſtrong;
Cryd ' Whar is Hardyknute ſae famd,   235
  ' And feird at Britain's throne?
' Tho Britons tremble at his name,
  ' I ſune fall mak him wail,
' That eir my ſword was made ſae ſharp,
  ' Sae ſaft his coat of mail.'   240

That brag his ſtout heart cold na bide,
  It lent him youthfu micht:
" I'm Hardyknute. This day," he cryed,
  " To Scotland's king I hicht
" To lay thee law as horſe's huſe;   245
  " My word I mein to keip:"
Syne with the firſt dint eir he ſtrake
  He gar'd his body bleid.

Norſe ene like grey goſehauk ſtaird wilde,
  He ſich'd wi ſhame and ſpyte;   250
' Diſgrac'd is now my far famd arm
  ' That left thee pouir to ſtryke.'
Syne gied his helm a blow ſhe fell,
  It made him down to ſtoup,
Sae law as he to ladies us'd,   255
  In courtly gyſe to lout.

                          Full

Full fune he ras'd his bent body;
  His bou he marveld fair,
Sen blaws till than on him but dar'd
  As touch of Fairly fair.   260
Norfe ferlied too as fair as he,
  To fee his ftately luik;
Sae fune as eir he ftrake a fae,
  Sae fune his lyfe he tuke.

Whar, like a fyre to hether fet,   265
  Bauld Thomas did advance,
A fturdy fae, with luik enrag'd,
  Up towards him did prance.
He fpurd his fteid throuch thickeft ranks
  The hardy youth to quell;   270
Wha ftude unmuvit at his approach
  His furie to repell.

'That fhort brown fhaft, fae meinly trimd,
  'Lukes like poor Scotland's geir;
'But dreidfu feims the rufty point!' 275
  And loud he leuch in jeir.
"Aft Britons blude has dim'd it's fhyne
  "It's point cut fhort their vaunt."
Syne perc'd the bofter's bairded cheik
  Nae time he tuke to taunt.   280

Short

Short while he in his fadil fwang;
   His ftirrip was nae ftay,
But feible hang his unbent knie,
   Sair taken he was, fey!
Swyth on the hardend clay he fell,   285
   Richt far was heard the thud;
But Thomas luk'd not as he lay
   All waltering in his blude.

Wi careles gefture, mind unmuv'd,
   On rade he north the plain   290
His feim in peace, or fercest ftryfe,
   Ay recklefs, and the fame.
Nor yit his heart dames' dimpeld cheik
   Cold meife faft luve to bruik;
Till vengefu Ann returnd his fcorn,   295
   Then languid grew his luke.

In thrauis of dethe, wi wallow'd cheik,
   All panting on the plain,
The bleiding corps of warriours lay,
   Neir to arife again: 300
Neir to return to native land;
   Na mair wi blythfum founds
To boift the glories of that day,
   And fhaw their fhynand wounds.

                      On

On Norway's coaſt the widowd dame 305
  May waſh the rocks wi teirs,
May lang luke owr the ſhiples ſeas
  Before her mate appeirs.
Ceiſe, Emma, ceiſe to hope in vain,
  Thy lord lyes in the clay; 310
The valiant Scots na rievers thole
  To carry lyfe away.

There on a lee, whar ſtands a croſs
  Set up for monument,
Thouſands fu ferce, that ſummer's day, 315
  Fill'd kene wars black intent.
Let Scots while Scots praiſe Hardyknute
  Let Norſe the name aye dreid;
Ay how he faucht, aft how he ſpaird
  Sall lateſt ages reid. 320

Loud and chill blew the weſtlin wind,
  Sair beat the heavy ſhouir,
Mirk grew the nicht ere Hardyknute
  Wan neir his ſtately touir:
His touir that us'd wi torches bleiſe 325
  To ſhyne ſae far at nicht
Seim'd now as black as mourning weid
  Na marvel fair he ſich'd.

" There's na licht in my lady's bouir,
  " There's na licht in my ha;   330
" Na blynk fhynes round my Fairly fair,
  " Na ward ftands on my wa.
" What bodes it ? Robert, Thomas, fay."
  Na anfwer fits their dreid.
" Stand back my fons I'll be your gyde."   335
  But by they paft wi fpeid.

" As faft I ha fped owr Scotland's faes—"
  There ceis'd his brag of weir,
Sair fhamd to mind ocht but his dame,
  And maiden Fairly fair.   340
Black feir he felt, but what to feir
  He wift nae yit wi dreid:
Sair fhuke his body, fair his limbs
  And a the warriour flied.

PART

PART II.

" RETURN, return, ye men of bluid,
    " And bring me back my chylde!"
A dolefu voice frae mid the ha
    Reculd, wi echoes wylde.
Beftraught wi dule and dreid, na pouir
    Had Hardyknute at a;
Full thrife he raught his ported fpeir,
    And thrife he let it fa.

" O haly God, for his deir fake,
    " Wha favd us on the rude——
He tint his praier, and drew his glaive,
    Yet reid wi Norland bluid.
" Brayd on, brayd on, my ftalwart fons,
    " Grit caufe we ha to feir;
" But aye the canny ferce contemn
    " The hap they canna veir."

' Return, return, ye men of bluid,
    ' And bring me back my chylde!'
The dolefu voice frae mid the ha
    Reculd, wi echoes wylde.
The ftorm grew rife, throuch a the lift
    The rattling thunder rang,
The black rain fhour'd, and lichtning glent
    Their harnifine alang.

What feir poffeft their boding breefts   25
    Whan, by the gloomy glour,
The caftle ditch wi deed bodies
    They faw was filled out owr!
Quoth Hardyknute " I wold to Chryfte
    " The Norfe had wan the day,   30
" Sae I had keipt at hame but anes,
    " Thilk bluidy feats to ftay."

Wi fpeid they paft, and fune they recht
    The bafe-courts founding bound,
Deip groans fith heard, and throuch the mirk
    Lukd wiftfully around.
The moon, frae hind a fable cloud,
    Wi fudden twinkle fhane,
Whan, on the cauldrif eard, they fand
    The gude Sir Mordac layn.   40

Befprent wi gore, fra helm to fpur,
    Was the trew-heartit knicht;
Swith frae his fteid fprang Hardyknute
    Muv'd wi the heavy ficht.
" O fay thy mafter's fhield in weir,   45
" His fawman in the ha,
" What hatefu chance cold ha the pouir
    " To lay thy eild fae law?"

To his complaint the bleiding knicht
 Returnd a piteous mane,
And recht his hand, whilk Hardyknute
 Claucht ftrcitly in his ain:
' Gin eir ye fee lord Harkyknute,
 ' Frae Mordac ye maun fay,
' Lord Draffan's treafoun to confute 55
 ' He ufd his fteddieft fay.'

He micht na mair, for cruel dethe
 Forbad him to proceid:
" I vow to God, I winna fleip
 " Till I fee Draffan bleid. 60
" My fons your fifter was owr fair:
 " But bruik he fall na lang
" His gude betide; my laft forbode
 " He'll trow belyve na fang.

" Bown ye my eydent friends to kyth 65
 " To me your luve fae deir;
" The Norfe' defeat mote weil perfuade
 " Nae riever ye neid feir."
The fpeirmen, wi a michty fhout,
 Cryd ' Save our mafter deir! 70
' While he dow beir the fway bot care
 ' Nae reiver we fall feir.'

' Return,

' Return, return, ye men of bluid
  ' And bring me back my chylde !'
The dolefu voice frae mid the ha   75
  Reculd wi echoes wylde.
" I am to wyte my valiant friends :"
  And to the ha they ran,
The stately dore full streitly steiked
  Wi iron boltis thrie they fand.   80

The stately dore, thouch streitly steiked
  Wi waddin iron boltis thrie,
Richt fune his micht can eithly gar
  Frae aff it's hinges flie.
" Whar ha ye tane my dochter deir ?   85
  " Mair wold I fee her deid
" Than fee her in your bridal bed,
  " For a your portly meid.

" What thouch my gude and valiant lord
  " Lye strecht on the cauld clay ?   90
" My sons the dethe may ablins spair
  " To wreak their sisters wae.
" O my leil lord, cold I but ken
  " Where thy dear corse is layn,
" Fra gurly weit, and warping blast   95
  " I'd shield it wi my ain !

C 2   " Dreir

" Dreir dethe richt fune will end my dule,
   " Ye riever ferce and vile,
" But thouch ye flay me, frae my heart
   " His luve ye'll neir exile."   100
Sae did fhe crune wi heavy cheir,
   Hyt luiks, and bleirit eyne;
Then teirs firft wet his manly cheik
   And fnawy baird bedeene.

' Na riever here, my dame fae deir,   105
   ' But your leil lord you fee;
' May hieft harm betide his life
   ' Wha brocht fic harm to thee!
' Gin anes ye may beleive my word,
   ' Nor am I ufd to lie, '   110
' By day-prime he or Hardyknute
   ' The bluidy dethe fhall die."

The ha, whar late the linkis bricht
   Sae gladfum fhind at een,
Whar penants gleit a gowden bleife   115
   Our knichts and ladys fhene,
Was now fae mirk, that, throuch the bound,
   Nocht mote they wein to fee,
Alfe throuch the fouthern port the moon
   Let fa a blinkand glie.   120

" Are

" Are ye in fuith my deir luvd lord?"
  Nae mair fhe doucht to fay,
But fwounit on his harneft neck
  Wi joy and tender fay.
To fee her in fic balefu fort   125
  Revived his felcouth feirs;
But fune fhe raifd her comely luik,
  And faw his faing teirs.

" Ye are nae wont to greit wi wreuch,
  " Grit caufe ye ha I dreid;   130
" Hae a our fons their lives redemd
  " Frae furth the dowie feid?"
' Saif are our valiant fons, ye fee,
  ' But lack their fifter deir;
' When fhe's awa, bot any doubt,   135
  ' We ha grit caufe to feir.'

" Of a our wrangs, and her depart,
  " Whan ye the fuith fall heir,
" Na marvel that ye ha mair caufe,
  " Than ye yit weit, to feir.   140
" O wharefore heir yon feignand knicht
  " Wi Mordac did ye fend?
" Ye funer wald ha perced his heart
  " Had ye his ettling kend."

'What may ye mein my peirles dame?
　'That knicht did muve my ruthe
'We balefu mane; I did na dout
　'His curtesie and truthe.
'He maun ha tint wi sma renown
　'His life in this fell rief;　　　　　　　150
'Richt fair it grieves me that he heir
　'Met sic an ill relief.'

Quoth she, wi teirs that down her cheiks
　Ran like a silver shouir,
"May ill befa the tide that brocht　　　　155
　"That fause knicht to our touir:
"Ken'd ye na Draffan's lordly port,
　"Thouch cled in knichtly graith?
"Tho hidden was his hautie luik
　"The visor black benethe?"　　　　　　160

'Now, as I am a knicht of weir,
　'I thocht his seeming trew;
'But, that he sae deceived my ruthe,
　'Full fairly he sall rue.'
"Sir Mordac to the sounding ha　　　　165
　"Came wi his cative fere;"
'My syre has sent this wounded knicht
　'To pruve your kyndlie care.

　　　　　　　　　　　　　　'Your

' Your fell maun watch him a the day,
  ' Your maids at deid of nicht ;   170
' And Fairly fair his heart maun cheir
  ' As she stands in his ficht.'
" Nae suner was Sir Mordac gane,
  " Than up the featour sprang ;"
' The luve alse o your dochter deir   175
  ' I feil na ither pang.

' Tho Hardyknute lord Draffan's suit
  ' Refus'd wi mickle pryde ;
' By his gude dame and Fairly fair
  ' Let him not be denyd.'   180
" Nocht muvit wi the cative's speech,
  " Nor wi his stern command ;
" I treasoun ! cryd, and Kenneth's blade
  " Was glisterand in his hand.

" My son lord Draffan heir you see,   185
  " Wha means your sister's fay
" To win by guile, when Hardyknute
  " Strives in the irie fay."
' Turn thee ! thou riever Baron, turn !'
  " Bauld Kenneth cryd aloud ;   190
" But, sune as Draffan spent his glaive,
  " My son lay in his bluid."

                                ' I did

'I did nocht grein that bluming face
  'That dethe fac fune fold pale;
'Far lefs that my trew luve, throuch me,   195
  'Her brither's dethe fold wail.
'But fyne ye fey our force to prive,
  'Our force we fall you fhaw!'
" Syne the fhrill-founding horn bedeen
  " He tuik frae down the wa.   200

" Ere the portculie cold be flung,
  " His kyth the bafe-court fand;
" Whan fcantly o their count a teind
  " Their entrie micht gainftand.
" Richt fune the raging rievers ftude   205
  " At their faufe mafter's fyde,
" Wha, by the haly maiden, fware
  " Na harm fold us betide.

" What fyne befell ye weil may guefs,
  " Reft o our eilds delicht."   210
'We fall na lang be reft, by morne
  'Sall Fairly glad your ficht.
'Let us be gane my fons, or now
  'Our meny chide our ftay;
'Fareweil my dame; your dochter's luve   215
  'Will fune cheir your effray.'

                                        Then

Then pale pale grew her teirfu cheik;
 " Let ane o my fons thrie
" Alane gyde this emprize, your eild
 " May ill fic travel drie. 220
" O whar were I, were my deir lord,
 " And a my fons, to bleid!
" Better to bruik the wrang than fae
 " To wreak the hie mifdede.

The gallant Rothfay rofe bedeen 225
 His richt of age to pleid;
And Thomas fhawd his ftrenthy fpeir;
 And Malcolm mein'd his fpeid.
' My fons your ftryfe I gladly fee,
 ' But it fall neir be fayne, 230
' That Hardyknute fat in his ha,
 ' And heird his fon was flayne.

' My lady deir, ye neid na feir;
 ' The richt is on our fyde:'
Syne rifing with richt frawart hafte 235
 Nae parly wald he byde.
The lady fat in heavy mude,
 Their tunefu march to heir,
While, far ayont her ken, the found
 Na mair mote roun her eir. 240

O ha

O ha ye fein fum glitterand touir,
   Wi mirrie archers crownd,
Wha vaunt to fee their trembling fae
   Keipt frae their countrie's bound?
Sic aufum ftrenth fhawd Hardyknute;   245
   Sic feimd his ftately meid;
Sic pryde he to his meny bald,
   Sic feir his faes he gied.

Wi glie they paft our mountains rude,
   Owr muirs and moffes weit;   250
Sune as they faw the rifing fun,
   On Draffan's touirs it gleit.
O Fairly bricht I marvel fair
   That featour eer ye lued,
Whafe treafoun wrocht your father's bale,   255
   And fhed your brither's blude!

The ward ran to his youthfu lord,
   Wha fleipd his bouir intill:
' Nae time for fleuth, your raging faes
   ' Fare doun the weftlin hill.   260
' And, by the libbard's gowden low
   ' In his blue banner braid,
' That Hardyknute his dochtir feiks,
   ' And Draffans dethe, I rede.'

                                        " Say

"Say to my bands of matchlefs micht, 265
   " Wha camp law in the dale,
" To bufk their arrows for the fecht,
   " And ftreitly gird their mail.
" Syne meit me here, and wein to find
   " Nae juft or turney play; 270
" Whan Hardyknute braids to the field,
   " War bruiks na lang delay."

His halbrik bricht he brac'd bedeen;
   Fra ilka fkaith and harm
Securit by a warloc auld, 275
   Wi mony a fairy charm.
A feimly knicht cam to the ha:
   ' Lord Draffan I thee braive,
' Frae Hardyknute my worthy lord,
   ' To fecht wi fpeir or glaive. 280

" Your hautie lord me braives in vain
   " Alane his micht to prive,
" For wha, in fingle feat of weir,
   " Wi Hardyknute may thrive?
" But fith he meins our ftrenth to fey, 85
   " On cafe he fune will find,
" That thouch his bands leave mine in ire,
   " In force they're far behind.

"Yet cold I wete that he wald yield
  "To what bruiks nae remeid,   290
"I for his dochter wald nae hain
  "To ae half o my fteid."
Sad Hardyknute apart frae a
  Leand on his birnift fpeir;
And, whan he on his Fairly deimd,   295
  He fpar'd nae fich nor teir.

"What meins the felon cative vile?
  "Bruiks this reif na remeid?
"I fcorn his gylefu vows ein thouch
  "They recht to a his fteid."   300
Bownd was lord Draffan for the fecht,
  Whan lo! his Fairly deir
Ran frae her hie bouir to the ha
  Wi a the fpeid of feir.

Ein as the rudie ftar of morne   305
  Peirs throuch a cloud of dew,
Sae did fhe feim, as round his neck
  Her fnawy arms fhe threw.
'O why, O why, did Fairly wair
  'On thee her thouchtles luve?   310
'Whafe cruel heart can ettle aye
  'Her father's dethe to pruve!'

                                           And

And first he kifsd her bluming cheik,
   And fyne her bofom deir;
Than fadly ftrade athwart the ha,
   And drapd ae tendir teir.
" My meiny heid my words wi care,
   " Gin ony weit to flay
" Lord Hardyknute, by hevin I fweir
   " Wi lyfe he fall nae gae."

' My maidens bring my bridal gowne,
   ' I little trewd yeftrene,
' To rife frae bonny Draffan's bed,
   ' His bluidy dethe to fene.'
Syne up to the hie baconie
   She has gane wi a her train,
And fune fhe faw her ftalwart lord
   Attein the bleifing plain.

Owr Nethan's weily ftreim he fared
   Wi feeming ire and pryde;
His blafon, glifterand owr his helm,
   Bare Allan by his fyde.
Richt fune the bugils blew, and lang
   And bludy was the fray;
Eir hour of nune, that elric tyde,
   Had hundreds tint their day.

Like beacon bricht at deid of nicht,
   The michty chief muvd on;
His basnet, bleising to the sun,
   Wi deidly lichtning shone.
Draffan he socht, wi him at anes 340
   To end the cruel stryfe;
But aye his speirmen thranging round
   Forfend their leider's lyfe.

The winding Clyde wi valiant bluid 345
   Ran reiking mony a mile;
Few stude the faucht, yet dethe alane
   Cold end their irie toil.
' Wha flie, I vow, sall frae my speir
   ' Receive the dethe they dreid!' 35
Cryd Draffan, as alang the plain
   He spurd his bluid-red steid.

Up to him sune a knicht can prance,
   A graith'd in silver mail:
" Lang have I socht thee throuch the field, 355
   " This lance will tell my tale."
Rude was the fray, till Draffan's skill
   Oercame his youthfu micht;
Perc'd throuch the visor to the eie
   Was slayne the comly knicht.
                                     36

The visor on the speir was deft,
   And Draffan Malcolm spied;
' Ye should your vaunted speid this day,
   ' And not your strenth, ha sey'd.'
" Cative, awa ye maun na flie,"   365
   Stout Rothsay cry'd bedeen,
" Till, frae my glaive, ye wi ye beir
   " The wound ye fein'd yestrene."

' Mair o your kins bluid ha I spilt
   ' Than I docht evir grein;   370
' See Rothsay whar your brither lyes
   ' In dethe afore your eyne.'
Scant Rothsay stapt the faing teir;
   " O hatefu ursed deid!
" Sae Draffan seiks our sister's luve,   375
   " Nor feirs far ither meid!"

Swith on the word an arrow cam
   Frae ane o Rothsay's band,
And smote on Draffan's lifted targe,
   Syne Rothsays splent asound.   380
Perc'd throuch the knie to his force steid,
   Wha pranc'd wi egre pain,
The chief was forced to quit the stryfe,
   And seik the nether plain.

His minftrals there wi dolefu care 385
　　The bludy fhaft withdrew;
But that he fae was bar'd the fecht
　　Sair did the leider rue.
' Cheir ye my mirrie men,' Draffan cryd,
　　Wi meikle pryde and glie;
' The prife is ours; nae chieftan bides 390
　　' Wi us to bate the grie.'

That hautie boaft heard Hardyknute,
　　Whar he lein'd on his fpeir,
Sair weiried wi the nune-tide heat, 395
　　And toilfum deids of weir.
The firft ficht, whan he paft the thrang,
　　Was Malcolm on the fwaird:
" Wold hevin that dethe my eild had tane,
　　" And thy youtheid had fpard! 400

" Draffan I ken thy ire, but now
　　" Thy micht I mein to fee!"
But eir he ftrak the deidly dint
　　The fyre was on his knie.
' Lord Hardyknute ftryke gif ye may, 405
　　' I neir will ftryve wi thee;
' Forfend your dochter fee you flayne
　　' Frae whar fhe fits on hie!

' Yeftrene

' Yeſtrene the prieſt in haly band
  ' Me joind wi Fairly deir ;   410
' For her ſake let us part in peace,
  ' And neir meet mair in weir.'
" Oh king of hevin, what ſeimly ſpeech
  " A featour's lips can ſend !
" And art thou he wha baith my ſons   415
  " Brocht to a bluidy end ?

" Haſte, mount thy ſteid, or I fall licht
  " And meit thee on the plain ;
" For by my forbere's ſaul we neir
  " Sall part till ane be ſlayne."   420
' Now mind thy aith,' fyne Draffan ſtout
  To Allan leudly cryd,
Wha drew the ſhynand blade bot dreid
  And perc'd his maſters ſyde.

Law to the bleiding eard he fell,   425
  And dethe ſune clos'd his eyne.
" Draffan, till now I did na ken
  " Thy dethe cold muve my tein.
" I wold to Chryſte thou valiant youth,
  " Thou wert in life again ;   430
" May ill befa my ruthles wrauth
  " That brocht thee to ſic pain !

                D   " Fairly,

" Fairly, anes a my joy and pryde,
  " Now a my grief and bale,
" Ye maun wi haly maidens byde   435
  " Your deidly faut to wail.
" To Icolm beir ye Draffan's corfe,
  " And dochter anes fae deir,
" Whar fhe may pay his heidles luve
  " Wi mony a mournfu teir."   440

                                    H. CHILD

II. CHILD MAURICE.

CHILD MAURICE was an erle's son,
 His name it waxed wide;
It was nae for his great riches,
 Nor yit his meikle pride,
But for his dame, a lady gay
 Wha livd on Carron fide.

' Whar fall I get a bonny boy,
 ' That will win hofe and fhoen,
' That will gae to lord Barnard's ha,
 ' And bid his lady come ?   10

' And ye maun rin errand Willie,
 ' And ye maun rin wi fpeid;
' When ither boys gang on their feet
 ' Ye fall ha prancing fteid.'

" O no! oh no! my mafter deir!
 " I dar na for my life;
" I'll no gae to the bauld barons,
 " For to trieft furth his wife."

' My bird Willie, my boy Willie,
 ' My deir Willie, he faid,   20
' How can ye ftrive againft the ftreim?
 ' For I fall be obeyd.'

          " But

" But O my mafter deir ! he cryd,
    " In grenewode ye're your lane;
" Gi owr fic thochts I wald ye red,   25
    " For feir ye fold be tane."

' Hafte, hafte, I fay, gae to the ha,
    ' Bid her come here wi fpeid;
' If ye refufe my hie command,
    ' I'll gar your body bleid.   30

' Gae bid her tak this gay mantel,
    ' 'Tis a gowd but the hem;
' Bid her come to the gude grenewode,
    ' Ein by herfel alane:

' And there it is, a filken farke,   35
    ' Her ain hand fewd the fleeve;
' And bid her come to Child Maurice;
    ' Speir nae bauld baron's leive.'

" Yes I will gae your black errand,
    " Thouch it be to your coft;   40
" Sen ye will nae be warnd by me,
    " In it ye fall find froft.

" The baron he's a man o micht,
    " He neir cold bide to taunt:
" And ye will fee before its nicht,   45
    " Sma caufe ye ha to vaunt.

                                    " And

" And fen I maun your errand rin,
   " Sae fair againſt my will,
" I'fe mak a vow, and keip it trow,
   " It fall be done for ill."   50

Whan he cam to the broken brig,
   He bent his bow and fwam;
And whan he came to grafs growing,
   Set down his feet and ran.

And whan he cam to Barnards yeat,   55
   Wold neither chap nor ca,
But fet his bent bow to his breiſt,
   And lichtly lap the wa.

He wald na tell the man his errand
   Thoch he ſtude at the yeat;   60
But ſtreight into the ha he cam,
   Whar they were fet at meat.

' Hail! hail! my gentle fire and dame!
   ' My meſſage winna wait,
' Dame ye maun to the grenewode gae,   65
   ' Afore that it be late.

' Ye're bidden tak this gay mantel,
   ' Tis a gowd bot the hem:
' Ye maun haſte to the gude grenewode,
   ' Ein by yourſell alane.

D 3   ' And

'And there it is, a silken sark,
  'Your ain hand sewd the sleive;
'Ye maun gae speik to Child Maurice;
  'Speir na bauld baron's leive.'

The lady stamped wi her foot, 75
  And winked wi her eie;
But a that she cold say or do,
  Forbidden he wald nae be.

"It's surely to my bower-woman,
  "It neir cold be to me." 80
'I brocht it to lord Barnard's lady,
  'I trow that ye be she.'

Then up and spak the wylie nurse,
  (The bairn upon her knie),
"If it be come from Child Maurice 85
  "It's deir welcum to me."

'Ye lie, ye lie, ye filthy nurse,
  'Sae loud as I heir ye lie;
'I brocht it to lord Barnard's lady
  'I trow ye be nae shee.' 90

Then up and spake the bauld baron,
  An angry man was he:
He has tane the table wi his foot,
  Sae has he wi his knie,
Till cryftal cup and ezar difh
  In flinders he gard flie.

"Gae

" Gae bring a robe of your cliding,
    " Wi a the hafte ye can,
" And I'll gae to the gude grenewode,
    " And fpeik wi your lemman."   100

' O bide at hame now lord Barnard!
    ' I ward ye bide at hame;
' Neir wyte a man for violence,
    ' Wha neir wyte ye wi nane.'

Child Maurice fat in the grenewode,   105
    He whiftled and he fang:
" O what meins a the folk coming?
    " My mother tarries lang."

The baron to the grenewode cam,
    Wi meikle dule and care;   110
And there he firft fpyd Child Maurice,
    Kaming his yellow hair.

' Nae wonder, nae wonder, Child Maurice,
    ' My lady loes thee weil:
' The faireft part of my body   115
    ' Is blacker than thy heil.

' Yet neir the lefs now, Child Maurice,
    ' For a thy great bewtie,
' Ye'fe rew the day ye eir was born;
    ' That head fall gae wi me.'   120

Now he has drawn his trufty brand,
    And flaided owr the ftrae;
And throuch Child Maurice fair body
    He gar'd the cauld iron gae.

And he has tane Child Maurice heid,   125
    And fet it on a fpeir;
The meineft man in a his train,
    Has gotten that heid to beir.

And he has tane Child Maurice up,
    Laid him acrofs his fteid;   130
And brocht him to his painted bower
    And laid him on a bed.

The lady on the caftle wa
    Beheld baith dale and down;
And there fhe faw Child Maurice heid   135
    Cum trailing to the toun.

" Better I loe that bluidy heid,
    " Bot and that yellow hair,
" Than lord Barnard and a his lands
    " As they lig here and there."   140

And fhe has tane Child Maurice heid,
    And kiffed baith cheik and chin;
" I was anes fow of Child Maurice
    " As the hip is o the ftane.

        " I gae

" I gat ye in my father's houfe 145
  " Wi meikle fin and fhame;
" I brocht ye up in the grenewode
  " Ken'd to myfell alane:

" Aft have I by thy craddle fitten,
  " And fondly fein thee fleip; 150
" But now I maun gae 'bout thy grave
  " A mother's teirs to weip."

Again fhe kifs'd his bluidy cheik,
  Again his bluidy chin;
" O better I loed my fon Maurice, 155
  " Than a my kyth and kin!"

' Awa, awa, ye ill woman,
  ' An ill dethe may ye die!
' Gin I had ken'd he was your fon
  ' He had neir been flayne by me.' 160

" Obraid me not, my lord Barnard!
  " Obraid me not for fhame!
" Wi that fam fpeir, O perce my heart,
  " And fave me frae my pain!

" Since naething but Child Maurice head 165
  " Thy jealous rage cold quell
" Let that fame hand now tak her lyfe,
  " That neir to thee did ill.

                                    " To

" To me nae after days nor nichts
   " Will eir be saft or kind:
" I'll fill the air wi heavy sichs,
   " And greit till I be blind."

' Eneuch of bluid by me's been spilt,
   ' Seek not your dethe frae me;
' I'd rather far it had been mysel,
   ' Than either him or thee.

' Wi hopelefs wae I hear your plaint,
   ' Sair, fair, I rue the deid.—
' That eir this curfed hand of mine
   ' Sold gar his body bleid!

' Dry up your teirs, my winfome dame,
   ' They neir can heal the wound;
' Ye fee his heid upon the fpeir,
   ' His heart's bluid on the ground.

' I curfe the hand that did the deid,
   ' The heart that thocht the ill,
' The feet that bare me wi fic fpeid,
   ' The comlie youth to kill.

' I'll aye lament for Child Maurice
   ' As gin he war my ain;
' I'll neir forget the dreiry day
   ' On which the youth was flain.'

III. ADAM O GORDON.

IT fell about the Martinmas,
  Whan the wind blew fhrill and cauld:
Said Adam o Gordon to his men,
  " We maun draw to a hauld.

" And what a hauld fall we draw to,   5
  " My mirrie men and me?
" We will gae ftrait to Towie houfe
  " And fee that fair ladie."

The lady on her caftle wa
  Beheld baith dale and down,   10
When fhe was ware of a hoft of men
  Riding toward the toun.

' O fee ye not, my mirry men a,
  ' O fee ye not what I fee?
' Methinks I fee a hoft of men,   15
  ' I marvel wha they be.'

                                          She

She wein'd it had been her luvely lord,
   As he came ryding hame;
It was the traitor Adam o Gordon,
   Wha reck'd nae fin or fhame.

She had nae funer bufked herfel,
   And putten on her gown,
Than Adam o Gordon and his men
   Were round about the toun,

The lady ran to hir touir heid
   Sae faft as fhe cold dric,
To fee if by her fpeiches fair
   She cold wi him agree.

But whan he faw the lady fafe,
   And the yates a locked faft,
He fell into a rage of wrauth,
   And his heart was all aghaft.

" Cum doun to me ye lady gay,
   " Cum doun, Cum doun to me :
" This nicht ye fall lye in my arms,
   " The morrow my bride fall be."

' I winna cum doun ye faufe Gordon,
   ' I winna cum doun to thee;
' I winna forfake my ain deir lord,
   ' Thouch he is far frae me.'

" Give owr your houfe, ye lady fair,
    " Give owr your houfe to me;
" Or I fall brin yourfel therein,
    " Bot and your babies thrie."

' I winna give owr, ye faufe Gordon,   45
    ' To nae fic traitor as thee;
' And if ye brin me and my babes,
    ' My lord fall mak ye drie.

' But reach my piftol, Glaud my man,
    ' And charge ye weil my gun,   50
' For, bot if I perce that bluidy butcher,
    ' We a fall be undone.'

She ftude upon the caftle wa
    And let twa bullets flie;
She mift that bluidy butchers heart,   55
    And only razd his knie.

" Set fire to the houfe," cryd faufe Gordon,
    A wood wi dule and ire;
" Faufe lady ye fall rue this deid
    " As ye brin in the fire."   60

' Wae worth, wae worth ye Jock my man,
    ' I paid ye weil your fee;
' Why pow ye out the ground-wa ftane
    ' Lets in the reik to me?

                                        ' And

' And ein wae worth ye Jock my man
  ' I paid ye weil your hire;
' Why pow ye out the ground wa ſtane
  ' To me lets in the fire?'

" Ye paid me weil my hire, lady,
  " Ye paid me weil my fee:
" But now I'm Adam o Gordon's man;
  " And maun or doe or die."

O than beſpak her little ſon
  Frae aff the nourceʼs knie,
' Oh mither deir, gi owr this houſe,
  ' For the reik it ſmithers me!'

" I wald gie a my gowd, my chyld,
  " Sae wald I a my fee,
" For ae blaſt o the weſtlin wind,
  " To blaw the reik frae thee."

O than beſpak her dochter deir,
  She was baith jimp and ſma,
' O row me in a pair o ſheits,
  ' And tow me owr the wa.'

They rowd her in a pair o ſheits,
  And towd her our the wa,
But on the point o Gordon's ſpeir,
  She gat a deidly fa.

O bonnie bonnie was her mouth, 90
   And chirry were her cheiks;
And cleir cleir was her yellow hair,
   Wharon the red bluid dreips!

Than wi his speir he turnd her owr—
   O gin her face was wan! 95
Quoth he," ye are the first that eir
   " I wishd alive again."

He turnd her our and our again—
   O gin her skin was white!
" I micht ha spair'd that bonny face 100
   " To hae been sum mans delyte.

" Busk and bown, my mirry men a,
   " For ill doom I do guess:
" I canna luik on that bonnie face,
   " As it lyes on the grass." 105

' Wha luik to freits, my master deir,
   ' Freits will ay follow them:
' Let it neir be said, Adam o Gordon
   ' Was daunted by a dame.'

But whan the lady saw the fire 110
   Cum flaming our her heid,
She weip'd, and kist her children twain;
   " My bairns we been but deid."

The Gordon than his bugil blew,
    And faid, 'Awa, awa:
'Sen Towie Houfe is a in a flame,
    'I hauld it time to ga.'

O than befpied her ain deir lord,
    As he cam owr the lee;
He faw his caftle a in a blaze
    Sae far as he cold fee.

Then fair, O fair, his mind mifgave,
    And a his heart was wae;
"Put on, put on, my wichty men,
    "Sae faft as ye can gae.

"Put on, put on, my wichty men,
    "Sae faft as ye can drie;
"He that is hindmoft o the thrang
    "Sall neir get gude o me."

Than fum they rode, and fum they ran,
    Fu faft owtowr the bent,
But eir the formoft could win up
    Baith lady and babes were brent.

He wrang his hands, he rent his hair,
    And weipt in teinfu mude:
"Ah traitors, for this cruel deid
    "Ye fall weip teirs o bluid!"

And after the Gordon he has gane,
  Sae faft as he micht drie :
And fune in his foul hartis bluid
  He has wreken his deir ladie.

IV. SIR HUGH;

Or, the JEW's DAUGHTER.

THE bonnie boys o merry Lincoln
  War playin at the ba;
And wi them ftude the fweet Sir Hugh,
  The flower amang them a.

He kepped the ba there wi his foot,   5
  And catchd it wi his knie,
Till in at the cruel Jew's window
  Wi fpeid he gard it flie.

' Caft out the ba to me, fair maid,
  ' Caft out the ba to me:'—   10
" Ye neir fall hae't my bonnie Sir Hugh,
  " Till ye come up to me.

" Cum up fweet Hugh, cum up dear Hugh
  " Cum up and get the ba;"
' I winna cum up, I winna cum up   15
  ' Without my playferes a.'

And fhe has gane to her father's garden
  Sae faft as fhe cold rin;
And powd an apple red and white
  To wyle the young thing in.   20

                                        She

She wyld him fune throuch ae chamber,
  And wyld him fune throuch twa;
And neift they cam to her ain chamber,
  The faireft o them a.

She has laid him on a dreffin board,   25
  Whar fhe was ufd to dine;
And ftack a penknife to his heart,
  And drefs'd him like a fwine.

She row'd him in a cake o lead,
  And bade him lye and fleip;   30
Syne threw him in the Jew's draw-well,
  Fu fifty fathom deip.

Whan bells were rung, and mafs was fung,
  And ilka lady gaed hame;
Than ilka lady had her young fon,   35
  But lady Helen had nane.

She row'd her mantel her about,
  And fair fair can fhe weip;
She ran wi fpeid to the Jew's caftel,
  When a war faft afleip.   40

' My bonnie Sir Hugh, your mither calls,
  ' I pray thee to her fpeik:'
" O lady rin to the deip draw-well
  " Gin ye your fon wad feik."

Lady Helen ran to the deip draw-well, 45
 And kneel'd upon her knie;
' My bonnie Sir Hugh gin ye be here,
 ' I pray ye fpeik to me!'

" The lead is wondrous heavy mither,
 " The well is wondrous deip; 50
" A kene penknife fticks in my heart,
 " A word I dounae fpeik.

" Gae hame, gae hame, my mither deir,
 " Fetch me my winding fheet;
" For again in merry Lincoln toun 55
 " We twa fall never meit."

V. FLOD-

V. FLODDEN FIELD;

Or, the FLOWERS of the FOREST.

I Have heard o lilting at the ewes milking,
Lasses a lilting eir the break o day;
But now I hear moaning on ilka green loaning,
Sen our bra foresters are a wed away.

At bouchts in the morning nae blyth lads are scorning,
The lasses are lonely, dowie, and wae;
Nae daffin, nae gabbing, but siching and sabbing;
Ilk ane lifts her leglen and hies her away.

At een in the gloming nae swankies are roaming,
'Mang stacks wi the lasses at bogle to play;
For ilk ane sits dreary, lamenting her deary;
The Flowers o the Forest, wha're a wed away.

In harst at the sheiring na yonkers are jeiring;
The bansters are lyart, runkled, and gray;
At fairs nor at preaching, nae wooing nae fleeching,
Sen our bra foresters are a wed away.

O dule for the order sent our lads to the border!
The English for anes by gyle wan the day.
The Flowers o the Forest, wha ay shone the foremost,
The prime o the land lye cauld in the clay!

VI. EDWARD.

WHY does your brand sae drap wi bluid,
    Edward, Edward?
Why does your brand sae drap with bluid,
  And why sae sad gang ye O!
O I hae killd my hauk sae gude,   5
    Mither, mither:
O I hae killd my hauk sae gude;
  And I had nae mair but he, O!

Your haukis bluid was nevir sae reid,
    Edward, Edward.   10
Your haukis bluid was nevir sae reid,
  My deir son I tell thee O!
I hae killd my reid roan steid,
    Mither, mither:
O I hae killd my reid roan steid   15
  That erst was fair and frie O!

Your steid was auld, and ye hae mair,
    Edward, Edward:
Your steid was auld, and ye hae mair,
  Sum ither dule ye drie, O!   20
O I hae killd my fadir deir,
    Mither, mither:
O I hae killd my fadir deir,
  Alas! and wae is me O!

          What

What penance will ye drie for that,   25
               Edward, Edward?
What penance will ye drie for that,
        My deir fon now tell me O!
I'll fet my feet in yonder boat,
               Mither, mither: 30
I'll fet my feet in yonder boat!
        And I'le fare owr the fea, O!

What will ye do wi touirs and ha,
               Edward, Edward?
What will ye do wi touirs and ha,   35
        That were fae fair to fee, O!
I'le let them ftand till they doun fa,
               Mither, mither:
I'le let them ftand till they doun fa,
        For heir I maunae be O!   40

What will ye leive to bairns and wife,
               Edward, Edward?
What will ye leive to bairns and wife,
        When ye gang owr the fea O!
The warld's room to beg throuch life,   45
               Mither, mither:
The warld's room to beg throuch life,
        For them I neir maun fee, O!

What will ye leive to your mither deir,
      Edward, Edward
What will ye leive to your mither deir,
  My deir son, now tell me O!
The curse of hell frae me sall ye beir,
      Mither, mither:
The curse of hell frae me sall ye beir,
  Sic counseils ye gied me, O!

VII. SIR PATRICK SPENCE.

THE King fits in Dunfermlin toun,
  Drinking the bluid-red wine:
" Whar fall I get a gude failor,
  " To fail this fhip o mine?"

Than up and fpak an eldern knicht, 5
  Wha fat at his richt knie;
' Sir Patrick Spence is the beft failor,
  ' That fails upon the fea.'

The king has written a braid letter,
  And figned it wi his hand; 10
And fent it to Sir Patrick Spence,
  Wha walked on the fand.

The firft line that Sir Patrick red,
  A leud lauch lauched he;
The neift line that Sir Patrick red, 15
  The teir blinded his eie.

" O wha can he be that has don
  " This deid o ill to me,
" To fend me at this time o yeir
  " To fail upo the fea? 20

" Mak

" Mak haſte, mak haſte, my mirry men a
 " Our gude ſhip ſails the morne."
' O ſay na ſae, my maſter deir,
 ' For I feir deidly ſtorm.

' I ſaw the new moon late yeſtrene,   25
 ' Wi the auld moon in her arm;
' And I fear, I fear, my maſter deir,
 ' That we will cum to harm.'

Our Scottiſh nobles were richt laith
 To weit their ſhyning ſhoen;   30
But lang or a the play was owr,
 They wat their heids aboon.

O lang lang may their ladies ſit
 And luik outowr the ſand,
Or eir they ſee the bonnie ſhip   35
 Cum ſailing to the land!

Mair than haf owr to Aberdour—
 It's fifty fathom deip—
Lyes gude Sir Patrick Spence for aye
 Wi the Scots lords at his feit.   40

VIII. LADY

VIII. LADY BOTHWELL'S LAMENT.

BALOW, my babe, lye ftill and fleip,
 It grieves me fair to fee thee weip;
If thou'lt be filent I'll be glad,
Thy maining maks my heart full fad;
Balow my boy, thy mither's joy;   5
Thy father breids me great annoy.

Whan he began to feik my luve,
And wi his facred words to muve;
His feining faufe, and flattering cheir,
To me that time did nocht appeir;   10
But now I fee that cruel he
Cares neither for my babe nor me.

Lye ftill, my darling, fleip a while,
And whan thou wakeft fweitly fmile;
But fmile nae as thy father did   15
To cozen maids: nay, God forbid,
What yet I feir, that thou fold leir
Thy father's heart and face to beir!

Be ftill, my fad one: fpare thofe teirs,
To weip whan thou haft wit and yeirs; 20
Thy griefs are gathering to a fum,
God grant thee patience when they cum;
Born to fuftain a mother's fhame,
A father's fall, a baftard's name.

  Balow, &c.

IX. THE EARL OF MURRAY.

YE Hielands and ye Lawlands
    O whar hae ye been?
They have slain the Earl of Murray
    And laid him on the green!

'Now wae be to you Huntly!   5
    ' O wharfore did ye sae?
' I bad you bring him wi you;
    ' But forbad you him to slay.'

He was a bra galant,
    And he rid at the ring;   10
The bonnie Earl of Murray
    He micht ha been a king.

He was a bra galant,
    And he playd at the ba;
The bonnie Earl of Murray   15
    Was the flower amang them a.

He was a bra galant,
    And he playd at the gluve;
The bonnie Earl of Murray
    He was the queen's luve.   20

O lang will his lady
    Look owr the castle downe,
Ere she see the Earl of Murray
    Cum sounding throuch the toun!

X. SIR JAMES THE ROSE.

O Heard ye o Sir James the Rose,
    The young heir o Buleighan?
For he has kill'd a gallant squire,
    Whase friends are out to tak him.

Now he has gane to the house o Mar,   5
    Whar nane might seik to find him;
To see his dear he did repair,
    Weining she wold befreind him.

' Whar are ye gaing Sir James,' she said,
    ' O whar awa are ye riding?'   10
" I maun be bound to a foreign land,
    " And now I'm under hiding."

" Whar sall I gae, whar sall I rin,
    " Whar sall I rin to lay me?
" For I ha kill'd a gallant squire,   15
    " And his friends seik to slay me."

' O gae ye doun to yon laigh house,
    ' I sall pay there your lawing;
' And as I am your leman trew,
    ' I'll meet ye at the dawing.   20

He

He turnd him richt and round about
   And rowd him in his brechan:
And laid him doun to tak a sleip,
   In the lawlands o Buleighan.

He was nae weil gane out o sicht,
   Nor was he past Milstrethen,
Whan four and twenty belted knichts
   Cam riding owr the Leathen.

' O ha ye seen Sir James the Rose,
   ' The young heir o Buleighan?
' For he has kill'd a gallant squire,
   ' And we are sent to tak him.'

" Yea, I ha seen Sir James,' she said,
   " He past by here on Monday;
" Gin the steed be swift than he rides on,
   " He's past the Hichts of Lundie."

But as wi speid they rade awa,
   She leudly cryd behind them;
" Gin ye'll gie me a worthy meid,
   " I'll tell ye whar to find him."

' O tell fair maid, and, on our band,
   ' Ye'se get his purse and brechan.'
" He's in the bank aboon the mill,
   " In the lawlands o Buleighan."

Than out and fpak Sir John the Graham, 45
  Who had the charge a keiping,
" It's neer be faid, my ftalwart feres,
  " We killd him whan a fleiping."

They feized his braid fword and his targe,
  And clofely him furrounded: 50
" O pardon! mercy! gentlemen,"
  He then fou loudly founded.

' Sic as ye gae fic ye fall hae
  ' Nae grace we fhaw to thee can.'
" Donald my man, wait till I fa, 55
  " And ye fall hae my brechan;
" Ye'll get my purfe thouch fou o gowd
  " To tak me to Loch Lagan."

Syne they tuke out his bleiding heart,
  And fet it on a fpeir; 60
Then tuke it to the houfe o Mar,
  And fhawd it to his deir.

' We cold nae gie Sir James's purfe,
  ' We cold nae gie his brechan,
' But ye fall ha his bleeding heart 65
  ' Bot and his bleeding tartan.'

" Sir James the Rofe, O for thy fake
  " My heart is now a breaking,
" Curs'd be the day, I wrocht thy wae
  " Thou brave heir of Buleighan! 70

Then

Then up she raise, and furth she gaes;
  And, in that hour o tein,
She wanderd to the dowie glen,
  And nevir mair was sein.

And she has tane the deidly drug
   And pàt it in his cup,
Whan they gaed to the gladsum ha,   45
   And sat them down to sup:
   And wi ill speid
   To bed he gied,
   And never mair raise up.

The word came to his father auld   50
   Neist day by hour of dyne,
That Woodhouselie had died yestrene,
   And his dame had held the wyne.
   Quoth he " I vow
   " By Mary now,   55
   " She sall meit sure propine."

Syne he has flown to our gude king,
   And at his feet him layne;
' O justice! justice! royal liege,
   ' My worthy son is slayne.   60
   ' His lady's feid
   ' Has wrocht the deid,
   ' Let her receive the paine.'

Sair muvit was our worthy king,
    And an angry man was he ;   65
' Gar bind her to the deidly ftake,
    ' And birn her on the lie :
    ' That after her
    ' Na bluidy fere
    ' Her recklefs lord may flee.'   70

" O wae be to ye, nourice,
    " An ill dethe may ye drie !
" For ye prepar'd the deidly drug
    " That gard my deiry die :
    " May a the paine   75
    " That I darraine
    " In ill time, licht on thee !

" O bring to me my goun o black,
    " My mantel, and my pall ;
" And gie five merks to the friars gray   80
    " To pray for my poor faul :
    " And ilka dame,
    " O gentle name,
    " Bewar o my fair fall."

XII. LORD

XII. LORD LIVINGSTON.

From Tradition.

'GRAITH my fwifteft fteid,' faid Livingfton,
  ' But nane of ye gae wi me;
' For I maun awa by myfel alane
  ' To the foot of the grenewode tree.

Up fpak his dame wi meikle fpeid. 5
  " My lord I red ye bide;
" I dreimd a dreiry dreim laft nicht:
  " Nae gude fall you betide."

' What freit is this, my lady deir,
  ' That wald my will gainftand?' 10
" I dreimd that I gaed to my bouir dore,
  " And a deid man tuke my hand."

' Suith dreims are fcant,' faid the proud baron,
  And leuch wi jearing glie;
' But for this fweit kifs my winfum dame 15
  ' Neift time dreim better o me.'

' For I hecht to meit with lord Rothmar,
  ' To chafe the fallow deer;
' And fpeid we weil, by the our o nune,
  ' We fall return bot feir.'

Frae his fair lady's ficht he ſtrave
  His ettling fae to hide ;
But frae the grenewode he came nae back,
  Sin eir that deidly tide.

For Rothmar met him there bot fail,   25
  And bluidy was the ſtrife ;
Lang eir the nunetide meſs was rung,
  They baith war twin'd o life.

' Forgie, forgie me, Livingſton !
  ' That I lichtly ſet by your dame;   30
' For ſurely in a the warld lives not
  ' A lady mair free frae blame.

' Accurſed be my lawles luve
  ' That wrocht us baith ſic tein !'
" As I forgie my freind anes deir,   35
  " Sae may I be forgien.

" Thouch ye my counſeil fold ha tane
  " The gait of gyle to efchew ;
" Yet may my faul receive ſic grace
  " As I now gie to you."   40

The lady in her mournfu bouir
  Sat wi richt heavy cheir,
In ilka ſough that the laigh wind gied
  She weind her deir lord to heir.

                                         Whan

Whan the fun gaed down, and mirk nicht came, 48
  O teirfu were her eyne!
' I feir, I feir, it was na for nocht
  ' My dreims were fae dowie yeftrene!'

Lang was the nicht, but whan the morn cam,
  She faid to her menie ilk ane; 50
' Hafte, faddle your fteids, and feik the grenewode,
  ' For I feir my deir lord is flain.'

Richt fune they fand their lord and Rothmar
  Deid in ilk ither's arm;
' I guefs my deir lord that luve of my name 55
  ' Alane brocht thee to fic harm.'

' Neir will I forget thy feimly meid,
  ' Nor yet thy gentle luve;
' For fevin lang yeirs my weids of black
  ' That I luvd thee as weil fall pruve.' 60

F 4   XIII. BIN-

XIII. BINNORIE.

From Tradition.

To preserve the tone, as well as the sense of this Ballad, the burden should be repeated through the whole, though it is here omitted for the sake of concisenes.

THERE were twa sisters livd in a bouir;
    Binnorie, O Binnorie!
Their father was a baron of pouir,
    By the bonnie mildams of Binnorie.
The youngest was meek, and fair as the May,   5
Whan she springs in the east wi the gowden day:
The eldest austerne as the winter cauld,
Ferce was her saul, and her seiming was bauld.
A gallant squire cam sweet Isabel to wooe;
Her sister had naething to luve I trow;   10
But filld was she wi dolour and ire,
To see that to her the comlie squire
Preferd the debonair Isabel:
Their hevin of luve of spyte was her hell.
Till ae ein she to her sister can say   15
" Sweit sister cum let us wauk and play."
They wauked up, and they wauked down,
Sweit sang the birdis in the vallie loun!

         Whan

Whan they cam to the roaring lin,
She drave unweiting Isabel in.   20
' O sister! sister! tak my hand,
' And ye sall hae my silver fan;
' O sister! sister! tak my middle
' And ye sall hae my gowden girdle.'
Sumtimes she sank, sumtimes she swam,   25
Till she cam to the miller's dam:
The miller's dochter was out that ein
And saw her rowing down the streim.
" O father deir! in your mil dam
" There is either a lady or a milk white swan!"   30
Twa days were gane whan to her deir
Her wraith at deid of nicht cold appeir:
' My luve, my deir, how can ye sleip,
' Whan your Isabel lyes in the deip?
' My deir, how can ye sleip bot pain,   35
' Whan she by her cruel sister is slain?'
Up raise he sune in frichtfu mude,
' Busk ye my meiny and seik the flude.'
They socht her up, and they socht her doun,
And spyd at last her glisterin gown: 40
They rais'd her wi richt meikle care;
Pale was her cheik, and grein was her hair!
' Gae, saddle to me my swiftest steid,
' Her fere, by my fae, for her dethe sall bleid.'
A page cam rinning out owr the lie,   45
" O heavie tydings I bring!" quoth he,

" My

" My luvely lady is far awa gane,
" We weit the fairy hae her tane:
" Her fifter gaed wood wi dule and rage,
" Nocht cold we do her mind to funge.   50
" O Ifabel! my fifter!" fhe wold cry,
' For thee will I weip, for thee will I die!'
" Till late yeftrene in an elric hour
" She lap frae aft the hicheft touir"——
' Now fleip fhe in peace!' quoth the gallant Squire, 55
' Her dethe was the maift that I cold require:
' But I'il main for thee my Ifabel deir,

     ' Binnorie, O Binnorie!
' Full mony a dreiry day, bot weir,
    ' By the bonnie mildams of Finnorie.'   60

XIV. THE DEATH OF MENTEITH.

From Tradition.

SHRILLY shriek'd the raging wind,
   And rudelie blew the blast;
Wi awfum blink, throuch the dark ha,
   The speidy lichtning past.

' O hear ye nae, frae mid the loch,
   ' Arise a deidly grane?
' Sae evir does the spirit warn,
   ' Whan we sum dethe maun mane.

' I feir, I feir me, gude Sir John,
   ' Ye are nae safe wi me:
' What wae wald fill my hairt gin ye
   ' Sold in my castle drie!"

" Ye neid nae feir, my leman deir,
   " I'm ay safe whan wi thee;
" And gin I maun nae wi thee live,
   " I here wad wish to die.

His man cam rinning to the ha
   Wi wallow cheik belyve:
' Sir John Menteith, your faes are neir,
   ' And ye maun flie or strive.

" What

" What count fyne leids the cruel knicht?"
  ' Thrie fpeirmen to your ane:
' I red ye flie, my mafter deir,
  ' Wi fpeid, or ye'll be flain.'

" Tak ye this gown, my deir Sir John   25
  " To hide your fhyning mail:
" A boat waits at the hinder port
  " Owr the braid loch to fail."

" O whatten a piteous fhriek was yon
  " That fough'd upo my eir?"   30
' Nae piteous fhriek I trow, ladie,
  ' But the rouch blaft ye heir.'

They focht the caftle, till the morn,
  Whan they were bown'd to gae,
They faw the boat turn'd on the loch,   35
  Sir John's corfe on the brae.

XV. LORD AIRTH's COMPLAINT.

From a MANUSCRIPT.

IF thefe fad thoughts could be exprefs'd,
  Wharwith my mind is now poffefs'd,
My paffion micht, difclos'd, have reft,
    My griefs reveal'd micht flie:
But ftill that minde which dothe forbere 5
To yield a groan, a fich, or teire,
May by it's prudence, much I fear,
    Encreafe it's miferie.

My heart which ceafes now to plaine,
To fpeke it's griefs in mournful ftraine, 10
And by fad accents eafe my paine,
    Is ftupefied with woe.
For leffer cares doe murne and crie,
Whyle greater cares are mute and die;
As iffues run a fountain drie, 15
    Which ftop'd wold overflow.

My fichs are fled; no teirs now rin,
But fwell to whelm my foul within,
How pítieful the cafe I'm in,
   Admire but doe not trie.
My croffes I micht juftly pruve,
Are common forrows far abuve;
My griefs ay in a circle muve,
   And will doe till I die.

XVI.

From Tradition.

I WISH I were where Helen lies!
Night and day on me she cries
    To bear her company.
O would that in her darksome bed
My weary frame to rest were laid
    From love and anguish free!

I hear, I hear the welcome sound
Break slowly from the trembling mound
    That ever calls on me:
Oh blessed virgin! could my power
Vye with my wish, this very hour
    I'd sleep death's sleep with thee!

A lover's sigh, a lover's tear,
Attended on thy timeless bier:
    What more can fate require?
I hear, I hear the welcome sound—
Yes, I will seek the sacred ground,
    And on thy grave expire.

The worm now tastes that rosy mouth,
Where glowed, short time, the smiles of youth;
    And in my heart's dear home,
Her snowey bosom, loves to lye.—
I hear, I hear the welcome cry!
    I come, my love! I come.

O life begone! thy irkſome ſcene
Can bring no comfort to my pain:
    Thy ſcenes my pain recall!
My joy is grief, my life is dead,
Since ſhe for whom I lived is fled;
    My love, my hope, my all.

Take, take me to thy lovely ſide,
Of my loſt youth thou only bride!
    O take me to thy tomb!
I hear, I hear the welcome ſound!—
Yes life can fly at ſorrow's wound.
    I come, I come, I come.

FRAGMENTS.

I.

AS I was walking by my lane,
   Atween a water and a wa;
There fune I fpied a wee wee man,
   He was the leaft that eir I faw.

His legs were fcant a fhathmonts length,
   And fma and limber was his thie;
Between his fhoulders was ae fpan,
   About his middle war but thrie.

He has tane up a meikle ftane,
   And flang't as far as I cold fee;
Ein though I had been Wallace wicht,
   I dought nae lift it to my knie.

' O wee wee man but ye be ftrang!
   ' Tell me whar may thy dwelling be?'
" I dwell beneth that bonnie bouir,
   " O will ye goe wi me and fee?"

On we lap and awa we rade,
  Till we cam to a bonny green ;
We lichted fyne to bait our fteid,
  And out there cam a ladie fheen.

Wi four and twentie at her back,
  A comly cled in gliftering green :
Thouch there the king of Scots had ftude,
  The warft micht weil ha been his quene.

On fyne we paft wi wondering cheir,
  Till we cam to a bonny ha ;
The roof was o the beaten gowd,
  The flure was o the cryftal a.

Whan we cam there wi wee wee knichts,
  War ladies dancing jimp and fma ;
But in the twinkle of an eie,
  Baith green and ha war clein awa.

* * * * * * * *

II. Earl

II.

Earl Douglas then wham nevir knicht
  Had valour mair nae courtefie,
Is now fair blam'd by a the land
  For lichtlying o his gay ladie.

* * * * *

' Gae little page, and tell my lord,
  ' Gin he will cum and dyne wi me,
' I'll fet him on a feat o gowd,
  ' And ferve him on my bended knie.'

* * * * *

' Now wae betide ye black Faftnefs,
  ' Bot and an ill deid may ye die!
' Ye was the firft and formoft man
  ' Wha pairted my true lord and me.'

* * * * *

III.

* * * * * * * *

She has called to her her bouir maidens,
  She has called them ane by ane:
" There lyes a deid man in my bouir,
  " I wish that he war gane."

They ha booted him and spurred him,
  As he was wont to ryde,
A hunting horn ty'd round his waist,
  A sharp sword by his syde.

Then up and spak a bonnie bird,
  That sat upo the trie;
' What hae ye done wi Earl Richard,
  ' Ye was his gay ladie?'

" Cum doun, cum doun, my bonnie bird,
  " And licht upo my hand;
" And ye shall hae a cage o gowd,
  " Whar ye hae but the wand."

' Awa, awa, ye ill woman!
  ' Nae cage o gowd for me;
' As ye hae done to Earl Richard,
  ' Sae wad ye doe to me.'

* * * * * *

IV.

See ye the caftle's lonelie wa,
   That ryfes in yon yle?
There Angus mourns that eir he did
   His fovereign's luve begyle.

* * * * * * *

' O will ye gae wi me, fair maid?
   ' O will ye gae wi me?
' I'll fet you in a bouir o gowd
   ' Nae haly cell ye'fe drie.'

" O meikle lever wald I gang
   " To bide for aye wi thee,
" Than heid the king my father's will,
   " The haly cell to drie.

" Sin I maun nevir fee nor fpeke
   " Wi him I luve fae deir,
" Ye are the firft man in the land
   " I wald cheis for my fere."

* * * * * * *

V.

Whar yon cleir burn fra down the loch
    Rins faftlie to the fea,
There latelie bath'd in hete o nune
    A fquire of valour hie.

He kend nae that the faufe mermaid
    There us'd to beik and play,
Or he had neir gane to the bathe,
    I trow, that dreirie day.

Nae funer had he deft his claiths,
    Nae funer gan to fwim,
Than up fhe rais'd her bonnie face
    Aboon the glittering ftreim.

' O comlie youth, gin ye will cum
    ' And be my leman deir,
' Ye fall ha pleafance o ilk fort,
    ' Bot any end or feir.

' I'll tak ye to my emraud ha
    ' Wi perles lichted round;
' Whar ye fall live wi luve and me,
    ' And neir by bale be found.

* * * * * * * *

NOTES.

NOTES.

HARDYKNUTE.

PART I.

HARDYKNUTE.] This name is of *Danish* extract, and fignifies *Canute the Strong*. *Hardy* in the original implies *ftrong*, not *valiant*; and though ufed in the latter fenfe by the Englifh, yet the Scots ftill take it in its firft acceptation. " The names in " Cunningham," fays Sir David Dalrymple, " are all " Saxon, as is the name of the country itfelf." Annals of Scotland, *an.* 1160, *note.* The *Danish* and *Saxon* are both derived from the old *Gothic*, and were

were fo fimilar, that an inhabitant of the one nation might underftand one of the other fpeaking in his proper tongue. From the names and whole tenor of this poem, I am inclined to think the chief fcene is laid in Cunningham; where likewife the *battle of Largs*, fuppofed to be that fo nobly defcribed in the firft part, was fought.

Ver. 5. *Britons.*] This was the common name which the Scots gave the Englifh anciently, as may be obferved in their old poets; and particularly *Blind Harry*, whofe teftimony indeed can only be relied on, as to the common language and manners of his time; his life of Wallace being a tiffue of the moft abfurd fables ever mingled.

V. 9. *Hie on a hill,* &c.] This neceffary caution in thofe times, when ftrength was the only protection from violence, is well painted by a contemporary French bard:

> Un chafteau fcay fur roche efpouvantable,
> En lieu venteux, la rive perilleufe,
> La vy tyrant feant à haute table,
> En grand palais, en fal plantureufe, &c.
>
> *D'Alliac, Eveque de Cambray.*

V. 12. *Knicht.*] Thefe knights were only military officers attending the earls, barons, &c. as appears from the hiftories of the middle ages. See Selden, *Tit.*

Tit. Hon. P. II. c. 5. The name is of Saxon origin, and of remote antiquity, as is proved by the following fragment of a poem on the Spanish expedition of Charles the Great, written at that period:

>*Sie zeſlugen ros unde man*
>*Mit ire ſcarfen ſpiezen;*
>*Thie gote moſen an theme plöte binnen uliezen:*
>*Ther ſite was under goten kneghten,*
>*Sic kunden wole vechten.* i. e.

>Occiderunt equos et viros
>Acutis suis haſtis;
>Deos opportuit sanguine fluere:
>Hic mos erat inter nobiles *milites*,
>Poterant optime pugnare.

>*MS. de Bello Car. M. Hiſp. apud Keyſler diſſ. de Cultu Solis, Freji, & Othini;* Halæ, 1728.

The oath which the ancient knights of Scotland gave at their inveſtiture is preſerved in a letter of Drummond of Hawthorden to Ben Jonſon, and is as follows:

I ſhall fortifie and defend the true holy Catholique and Chriſtian religion, preſently profeſſed, at all my power.

I ſhall be loyal and true to my Sovereign Lord the King his Majeſty; and do honour and reverence to all orders of chevalrie, and to the noble office of arms.

I ſhall

I shall fortifie and defend justice to the uttermost of my power, but feid or favour.

I shall never flie from the King's Majesty my Lord and Master, or his lieutenant, in time of battel or medly, with dishonour.

I shall defend my native country from all aliens and strangers at all my power.

I shall maintain and defend the honest adoes and quarrels of all ladies of honour, widows, orphans, and maids of good fame.

I shall do diligence, wherever I hear tell there are any traitors, murtherers, rievers, and masterful theeves and outlaws, that suppress the poor, to bring them to the law at all my power.

I shall maintain and defend the noble and gallant state of chevalrie with horses, harneses, and other knichtly apparel to my power.

I shall be diligent to enquire, and seek to have the knowledge of all points and articles, touching or concerning my duty, contained in the book of chevalrie.

All and sundry the premises I oblige me to keep and fulfill. So help me God by my own hand, and by God himself.

A curious account of the rise and progress of knighthood, and its influence on society, may be found in a learned and ingenious work lately published by Dr. Stewart, intitled, *A View of Society in Europe, or Enquiries concerning the History of Law, Government, and Manners.*

V. 16.

NOTES. 91

V. 16. *Emergard.*] In the common copies it is Elenor, and indeed in all the recitals I have heard; but in a late edition published with other Scottish songs at Edinburgh, 1776, it is rightly read as here. *Emergard,* or *Ermengarde,* was daughter of the Viscount of Beaumont, and wife of Malcolm IV. She died in 1233. As the name was uncommon, and of difficult pronunciation, the rehearsers seem to have altered it to *Elenor,* which has none of these defects.

V. 25. *Fairly.*] This name seems likewise of Saxon origin. There is a small island and a rivulet in Cunningham still called *Fairly isle* and *Fairly Burn.*

V. 43. *Twenty thousand glittering speirs,* &c.] This agrees with Buchanan's account, *Acho—viginti millia militum expulit.* lib. 7. Torfœus asserts this number of the Norwegians was left dead on the field.

V. 49. *Page*] The Pages in the periods of chivalry were of honourable account. The young warriors were first denominated *pages,* then *valets,* or *damoiseaux,* from which degree they reached that of *ecuyer,* or *squire,* and from this that of *knight.* See *Du Cange,* voc. *Valeti,* & *Domicellus. St. Palaye,* Mem. sur l'anc. Cheval. *P. J.*

V. 61. *He has tane a horn,* &c] The *horn,* or *bugil,* was anciently used by the Scots instead of the trumpet. They were sometimes richly ornamented, as appears from Lindsay's description of that of Sir Robert Cochran.

ran. "The horn he wore was adorned with jewels
"and precious stones, and tipped with fine gold at
"both ends." *Hist. of Scotland*, J. III.

V. 83. Westmoreland's *ferce heir*.] *Heir*, in the old
Scottish acceptation, seems derived from the Latin *herus*, and signifies not *apparent successor*, but *present lord*.
As in the following lines of *Blind Harry:*

Of Southampton he hecht baith heir and lord.
B. 7. c. 1.

Of Glocester the huge lord and heir.
B. 12. c. 1.

And in this of *Dunbar*,

Befoir *Mahoun* the heir of hell.

V. 107—172.] This minute description might lead
us to suspect, that a female hand had some part in this
composition. But, before our minstrel, Homer has shewn
himself an adept in the lady's dress. To the curious
remarks on the variation of the British habit, given us by
Mr. Walpole, in his *Anecdotes of Painting*, and Mr. Granger,
in his *Biographical History*, might be added the following notice from a reverend minister of the church of
Scotland. "About 1698 the women got a custome of
"wearing few garments: I myselfe have seen the young
"brisk ladies walking on the streets with masks on their
"faces, and with one onlie thin petticoat and their
"smoak; so thin that one would make a conscience of
"sweiring

" fweiring they were not naked." *Mifcellanies, by Mr. John Bell, minifter at Gladfmuir,* MS. pen. edit. *title* Apparel.

V. 112. *Save that of Fairly fair.*] Working at the needle, &c. was reckoned an honourable employment by the greateft ladies of thofe times. Margaret, the queen of Malcolm III. as we learn from her life written by *Turgot* her confeffor, employed the leifure hours of her ladies in this manner. See Lord Hails's *Annals of Scotland,* an. 1093.

V. 121. *Sir Knicht.*] "The addition *Sir* to the "names of knights was in ufe before the age of Ed- "ward I. and is from *Sire*, which in old French fignifies "*Seignieur* or Lord. Though applicable to all knights, "it ferved properly to diftinguifh thofe of the order "who were not barons." Dr. Stewart, *View of Society,* &c. Notes *on* fect. 4. chap. ii. p. 269.

V. 123—128. The cuftom of the ladies tending the wounded knights was common in thofe romantic ages. *Lydgate,* whofe ftory is ancient, but whofe manners are thofe of his own times, has an inftance in *The Story of Thebes,* part ii. Speaking of the daughter of Lycurgus and Tideus;

> To a chamber fhe led him up aloft
> Full well befeine, there in a bed right foft,
>
> Richly

NOTES.

> Richly abouten apparrailed
> With clothe of gold, all the floure irailed
> Of the fame both in length and brede:
> And firſt this lady, of her womanhede,
> Her women did bid, as goodly as they can,
> To be attendant unto this wounded man:
> And when he was unarmed to his ſhert,
> She made firſt waſh his woundis ſmert,
> And ſerch hem well with divers inſtruments,
> And made fet ſundrie ointments, &c.

And in an excellent piece of old Engliſh poetry, ſtyled Sir Cauline, publiſhed by Dr. Percy in the firſt volume of his *Reliques*, when the king is informed that knight is ſick, he ſays,

> Fetche me down my daughter deere,
> She is a leeche fulle fine.   v. 29, 30.

V. 145—152.] This ſtanza is now firſt printed. It is ſurpriſing it's omiſſion was not marked in the fragment formerly publiſhed, as without it the circumſtance of the knight's complaint is altogether foreign and vague. The loſs was attempted to be gloſſed over by many variations of the preceding four lines, but the defect was palpable to the moſt inattentive peruſer.

V. 154.

V. 154. *Lord Chattan.*] This is a very ancient and honourable Scottish surname. Some genealogists derive them from the *Chatti*, an ancient German tribe; but others, with more probability, from the *Gilchattan* of Ireland. St. *Chattan* was one of the first Scottish confessors, to whom was dedicated the priory of *Ardchattan* in Lorn, founded in 1230, and some others through the kingdom. The chief of the clan *Chattan* dying in the reign of David I. without male issue, the clan assumed the ancestor of the *M'Phersons* for superior, by which means the name appears to have been lost in that of *M'Pherson.* See *Buchanan's Brief Enquiry into the Genealogy and Present State of Ancient Scottish Surnames.* Glasgow, 1723, 4to, *p.* 67.

V. 159.] Though we learn from the last quoted author, that the clan *Chattan* are said to have come into Scotland long before the expulsion of the Picts, yet I do not find this pretty anecdote, which is much in the spirit of Homer, has any foundation in history. The empire of the Picts was demolished by Kenneth about four centuries before the apparent date of this poem.

V. 169. *Mak orisons,* &c.] This is perfectly in the style of knighthood. Before they entered into combat they solemnly invoked the aid of God, their Saviour, or their mistress: religion and gallantry being the prime motives of all their adventures. *Les premieres leçons*

leçons qu'on leur donnoit regardoient principalement l'amour de Dieu et des dames, c'est à dire la religion et la galanterie. St. Palaye, tome i. p. 7. The poets of these times began, in like manner, the description of a savage conflict, or of their lady's graces, with religious invocation. Many examples of which appear in the *Histoire des Troubadours* of L'Abbé Milot, and the *Specimens of Welsh Poetry* published by Mr. Evans. So blind is the untutored mind to the proper discrimination of it's ideas!

V. 179. *Play and Pibrochs.*] Of the *pibroch* I cannot give a better account than in the words of an excellent author. 'A pibroch is a species of tune pe-
' culiar, I think, to the Highlands and Western Isles of
' Scotland. It is performed on a bagpipe, and differs
' totally from all other music. Its rythm is so irregu-
' lar, and its notes, especially in the quick movement,
' so mixed and huddled together, that a stranger finds
' it almost impossible to reconcile his ear to it, so as to
' perceive its modulation. Some of these *pibrochs*, being
' intended to represent a battle, begin with a grave mo-
' tion resembling a march, then gradually quicken into
' the onset; run off with noisy confusion, and turbu-
' lent rapidity, to imitate the conflict and pursuit;
' then swell into a few flourishes of triumphant joy;
' and perhaps close with the wild and slow wailings of
' a funeral procession.' *Essays by Dr. Beattie*, 8vo ed. p. 422. *note.*

V. 188.

V. 188. *Eir faes their dint mote drie.*] This is substituted in place of a line of consummate nonsense, which has stained all the former editions. Many such are corrected in this impression from comparing different rehearsals, and still more from conjecture. When an ignorant person is desired to repeat a ballad, and is at a loss for the original expression, he naturally supplies it with whatever absurdity first occurs to him, that will form a rime. These the Editor made not the smallest scruple to correct, as he always imagined that common sense might have its use even in emendatory criticism.

V. 203. *But on his forehead*, &c.] The circumstances in this description seem borrowed from those of different battles betwixt the Kings of Scotland and Norway. I find in no historian that Alexander was wounded in the battle of Largs; on the contrary, it is even doubted whether he was present; but in that near *Nairn* Malcolm II. was wounded on the head. *Rex, accepto in capite vulnere, vix a suis in propinquum nemus ablatus, ac ibi equo positus, mortem evasit.* Buchan. lib. VI.

V. 223. *Hire dames to wail your darling's fall.*] This custom of employing women to mourn for the warriors who fell in battle, may be traced to the most distant antiquity. Lucilius, one of the earliest Roman poets, in a couplet preserved by Nonius, mentions this practise;

Mercede quæ conductæ flent alieno in funere præficæ
Multa & capillos scindunt, & clamant magis.

Among the Northern nations it partook of their barbarity. ' Inter eas autem ceremonias a barbara gente
' acceptas fuisse et has, ut genas roderunt mulierculæ,
' hoc est unguibus faciem dilaniarent et *lessum* facerent,
' id est sanguinem e venis mitterent, doloris testandi
' ergo; id quod Germani patria voce dicunt, *Ein lassu*
' *thun oder haben.*' Elias Schedius *de Diis Germ.* Syng. II.
c. 51. A similar mode of testifying their grief for the death of their chiefs, still obtains in the Highlands, as we are informed by Mr. Pennant in his amusing *Tour in Scotland*.

V. 225. *Costly Jupe.*] This was the *Sagum*, or military vest of the Gauls and Germans. Dr. Stewart has with curious ingenuity derived the science of Blazonry from the ornaments which were in time added to them. *Ubi supra*, p. 286, 287.

V. 229. *Beir Norse that gift*, &c.] This has been generally misunderstood: the meaning is, *Bear that gift to the King of Norway, and bid*, &c.

V. 239. 245.] These vaunts are much in Homer's manner, and are finely characteristic. The obscure metaphor which conveys them illustrates a beautiful remark of an ancient critic, That allegory has a sublime effect when applied to threatning. Μεγαλεῖον δέ τί ἐςιν καὶ ἡ Ἀλληγορία κ μάλιςα ἐν ταῖς ἀπειλαις· οἷον ὡς ὁ Διονύσιος ὅτι, " οἱ τέτλιγις αὐτοῖς ἄσονται χαμοθιν." Demet. Phal. de Eloc. c. 99.

V. 265.

V. 265. *Whar lyke a fyre to hether fet.*] This appofite fimile alludes to an ancient practice of the Scots, termed *Mure burning*. The progrefs of the flame was fo quick, that many laws appear in their Acts of Parliament, prohibiting its being ufed when any corn was ftanding on adjacent ground, though at a confiderable diftance from the fpot where the flame was kindled.

V. 285. *Sore taken he was, fey!*] *Fey* here fignifies only indeed, *in fay*, or, in faith: it is commonly ufed by the old Scottifh poets in a farcaftic or ironical fenfe.

V. 305. *On Norway's coaft*, &c.] Thefe verfes are in the fineft ftyle of Ballad poetry. They have been well imitated by a modern writer, who feems indebted, for the beft ftrokes of his firft production, to a tafte for fuch compofitions:

> Ye dames of Denmark! even for you I feel,
> Who fadly fitting on the fea-beat fhore,
> Long look for Lords that never fhall return.
> *Douglas*, Act III.

I cannot conclude my obfervations upon the defcription here given of the battle, without adding, that though perhaps not the moft fublime, it is the moft animated and interefting to be found in any poet. It yields not to any in Offian for lively painting, nor to any in Homer for thofe little anecdotes and ftrokes of nature, which are fo defervedly admired in that mafter. ' Poetry and Rhetoric,' fays the admirable author of an

Enquiry into the origin of our ideas of the Sublime and Beautiful, 'do not succeed in exact description so well 'as Painting does; their business is to effect rather by 'sympathy than imitation; to display rather the effect 'of things on the mind of the speaker, or of others, 'than to present a clear idea of the things themselves. 'This is their most extensive province, and that in 'which they succeed the best.' Will he forgive me if I offer this rude Scottish Poem as an example sufficiently illustrative of this fine remark?

V. 321. *Loud and chill blew the Westlin wind,* &c.] This storm is artfully raised by the magic of Poetry to heighten the terrible, which is soon carried to a degree not surpassed in any production ancient or modern. It will recall to the reader the like artifice employed in the most sublime passage of *Tasso's Gierusalemme*, end of Canto 7.; and of *Homer's Iliad*, VIII. ver. 161. of Mr. Pope's Translation.

V. 327. *Seimd now as black as mourning weid.*] It was anciently the custom on any mournful event to hang the castle gates with black cloth. This is alluded to here, and more particularly mentioned in an excellent modern Ballad, entitled *The Birth of St. George*, which displays no mean knowledge of the manners of chivalry;

 But when he reached his castle gate
 His gate was hung with black.
      Reliques, Vol. III. p. 222.

HARDYKNUTE. Part II.

I HAVE given the ftanzas now added the title of a Second Part, though I had no authority from the recital. The break formerly made here by accident feemed to call for this paufe to the reader.

V. 115. *Penants.*] Thefe were fmall banners charged with the arms of the owner, and fometimes borne over the helm of the ancient knight by his fquire, and, as would feem, even that of the Prince, Earl, or Chief Baron, by his Baneret. See ver. 331. The Englifh word is *penon:*

> And by his banner borne is his *penon*,
> Of gold full rich; in which there was ybete
> The minotaure than he wan in Crete,

Says Chaucer fpeaking of Thefeus in *The Knight's Tale.*

V. 252. *Draffan's touirs.*] The ruins of Draffan-caftle are in Lanarkfhire.—They ftand upon a vaft rock hanging over the *Nethan* (fee v. 329.) which a little below runs into the *Clyde.* From this a houfe fituated very nigh the ruins is called *Craignethan.* This caftle is fo ancient, that the country people there fay it was built by the *Péchts*, which is their common way of expreffing the *Picts.*

V. 273.

V. 273. *His halbrik.*] This term for a coat of mail occurs in *Blind Harry*. It was properly used for one composed of small rings of steel which yielded to every motion of the warrior, and was the same with the *lorica hamata* of the Romans, so picturesquely described by Claudian:

    Conjuncta per artem
Flexilis inductis hamatur lamina membris,
Horribilis visu, credas simulacra moveri
Ferrea, cognatoque viros spirare metallo.
        In Rufin. Lib. 2.

V. 275. *Securit by a warloc auld,* &c.] The belief that certain charms might secure the possessor from danger in combat was common in dark ages. ' I know ' a song, by which I soften and enchant the arms of my ' enemies, and render their weapons of no effect,' says *Odin* in his *Magic*. Northern Antiq. *Vol.* II. *p.* 217. Among the Longobards they were forbidden by a positive Law. ' Nullus Campio adversus alterum pugna-
' turus audeat super se habere *herbas nec res ad maleficia*
' *pertinentes*, nisi tantum corona sua, quæ conveniunt.
' Et si suspicio fuerit quod eas occulte habeat, inquira-
' tur per Judicem, et si inventæ fuerunt, rejiciantur.
' Post quam inquisitionem, extendet manum suam ipse
' in manu Patrini aut Colliberti sui, ante judicem,
' dicens, se nullam rem talem super se habere, deinde ad
' certamen prodeat.' *LL. Longob. apud L. Germ. J. Basil. Herold.* A similar notion obtained even in England,

as appears from the oath taken in the Judicial Combat.
' A. de B. ye shall swere that ye have no *stone of virtue*,
' *nor hearb of virtue, nor charme, nor experiment, nor none*
' *othir enchauntment by you nor for you, whereby ye trust*
' *the better to overcome C. de D. your adversarie*, that shall
' come agens you within these lists in his defence, nor
' that ye trust in none othir thynge propirly bot in
' God, and your body, and your brave quarel. So God
' you help and all halowes, and the holy gospells.' *Apud*
Dugdale, *Orig. Juridic. & Miscell. Aulica, Lond.* 1702.
p. 166. And we find in a most acute and ingenious
treatise on the point of honour, written in the middle of
the sixteenth century, that this precaution was esteemed
necessary so late as that period. *Il Duello del Mutio Justinopolitano*, In Vineg. 1566. lib. II. c. 9. *De i maleficii
et incante*. ' Et non senza ragione i moderni Padrini
' fanno spogliare i cavallieri, che hanno da entrare in
' battaglia, et iscuotere, et diligentemente essaminare
' i loro panni, &c.' Many instances occur in the accounts of the civil wars of France, and of the Netherlands; and more particularly in the very curious story
of *Gowrie's Conspiracy*, published by James VI. at *Edinburgh*, 1600, 4to. ' His Majesty having before his
' parting out of that towne, caused to search the sayde
' Earle of Gowries pockets, in case any letters that
' might further the discovery of that conspiracie might
' be founde therein. But nothing was found in them,
' but a little close parchment bag full of magical
' characters,

' characters, and wordes of enchantment, wherein it
' seemed that hee had put his confidence, thinking him-
' self never safe without them, and therefore ever car-
' ried them about with him; being also observed, that
' while they were upon him, his wound, whereof he
' died, bled not; but incontinent, after the taking of
' them away, the blood gushed out in great abundance,
' to the great admiration of all the beholders.' See
likewise *Memoirs of the Affairs of Scotland, by David
Moyses*, Edin. 1755. where this piece is reprinted *ver-
batim*. Maister William Rynd, a servant of Lord Gowrie's,
deposition in the same volume, *p*. 297, has singular
anecdotes with regard to these *characters*.

V. 276. Fairy *charm*.] The word *fairy* seems to have
been accepted by the ancient English and Scottish poets
for *supernatural*, or *enchanted*. So Chaucer speaking of
Cambuscan's horse,

It was of fairie, as the peple semed.

Squire's Tale, p. 1,

V. 362.] It was the priviledge of the knights to hide
their faces with armour, so that it was impossible to
distinguish any one from another, except by his *blazon*,
which seems at first to have been displayed over them,
but came at length to be painted on their shields,
whence *Coats of Arms*. A *villein* was obliged to have his
countenance uncovered in battle. This circumstance
attended to will save our wonder at Hardyknute's not
knowing

knowing Draffan in the Firſt Part, and Draffan's not perceiving Malcolm here till his ſpear tore off his viſor: though Rothſay knows Draffan either from his wearing a *blazon* on his armour, or from his face being uncovered in order to breathe from the combat.

V. 389. *Cheir ye my* mirrie men, &c.] It ſhould have been remarked on the firſt appearance of this word, P. I. v. 199, that *mirrie* was anciently uſed in a very different ſenſe from its preſent. It ſignified *honeſt*, *true*, *faithful*, but no where *jovial*. King James VI. in his *Dæmonologie* MS. *pen. Edit.* ' Surelie the difference vul-
' gaire put betwixt thame is verrie *mirrie*, *and in a man-*
' *ner trew.*' p. 10. And again in p. 18. ' Many *honeſt*
' *and mirrie* men.' In like manner Merlin's Prophecies are ſtiled ' *Mirrie words*,' in that of Beid. *Proph. of Rymer*, &c.

V. 413. *Oh King of Hevin!*] This is a common appellation of the Deity with the more ancient Scottiſh Poets. *Py Hevins King*, is the familiar oath of *Blind Harrie's* heroes.

V. 419. *By my Forbere's ſaul.*] Swearing by the ſouls of their anceſtors was another uſed mode in thoſe times. The greateſt thought this oath moſt ſtrong and honourable; probably becauſe it implied the ſouls of their forefathers were in heaven, and, as was then believed, might lend them a ſupernatural aid, if the intention of their oath was juſt and unblameable.

V. 421. ' *Now mind your aith*,' &c.] This paſſage is obſcure: the meaning I apprehend is, that Draffan
had,

had, before the combat, exacted an oath of Allan his baneret, that he would slay him, should the necessity of his affairs demand this sacrifice. More willing to lose his own life than possibly to take that of his great antagonist, he commands Allan to fulfill his engagement, which, with all the heroic faith of those times, he does without a pause. The particular expression ' *The* shynand ' blade' might lead us to imagine, that it was thought impossible to pierce the supposed enchanted armour, but with one particular weapon, likeways perhaps *charmed.*

V. 437. *Icolm.*] The Nunnery at Icolm, or Icolmkill, was one of the most noted in Scotland. The Nuns were of the order of *Augustine*, and wore a white gown, and above it a rocket of fine linen. *Spotiswood's Account of the Religious Houses in Scotland,* p. 509. The ruins of this nunnery are still to be seen, with many tombs of the Princesses; one of which bears the year 1000. *Martin's Western Islands,* p. 262.

I cannot conclude my remarks on this Poem without wasting one on the story of Mrs. Wardlaw. That this lady may have indeed received a MS. of it, as mentioned in Dr. Percy's introductory note, is highly probable. Many valuable MSS. prepared for the press, have had a worse fate. But that she was the author of this capital composition, so fraught with science of ancient manners as the above notes testify, I will no more credit, than that the common people in Lanarkshire,

who

who can repeat scraps of both the parts, are the authors of the passages they rehearse. That she did not refuse the name of being the original composer is a strange argument: would not the first poet in Europe think it added to his reputation? If conjecture may be allowed where proof must ever be wanting, I suspect, if we assign the end of the fifteenth century as the date of the antique parts of this noble production, we shall not greatly err; though at the same time the language must convince us, that many strokes have been bestowed by modern hands.

CHILD MAURICE.

THIS is undoubtedly the true title of this incomparable Ballad, though corrupted into Gil Morrice by the nurses and old women, from whose mouths it was originally published. *Child* seems to have been of equal importance with *Damoiseau* (See note on P. I. v. 49. of Hardyknute) and applicable to a young nobleman when about the age of fifteen. It occurs in Shakspeare's Lear, in the following line, probably borrowed from some old romance or ballad.

Child Roland to the dark tower came.
Act III. S. 7.

And in Chaucer's *Rime of Sir Topas*, *Child* is evidently used to denote a young and noble knight.
V. 52.

V. 52. *He bent his bow.*] Archery was enjoined the Scottish warrior at a very early age, as appears from many special laws to that effect, and particularly the following one of James I. 'Item, 'That all men busk 'them to be Archeres fra they be *twelfe yeir of age*, 'and that in ilk ten pundis worthe of lande their be 'maid bowmarkis, and speciallie neir to Paroche kirkis, 'quhairin upon haly daies men may cum, and at the 'leist schutte thrife about, and have usage of archerie: 'and quha sa usis not the said archerie, the Laird of 'the lande sall raise of him a wedder; and giff the Laird 'raises not the said payne, the King's schireffe or his 'ministers, shall raise it to the King.' *Parl.* I. § 18.

V. 107, 8. *O what means a the folk coming? My mother tarries lang.*] This stroke of nature is delicate. It paints the very thought of youth and innocence. In such happy *tenuity* of phrase, this exquisite composition is only rivalled by the *Merope* of *Maffei*, the most finished Tragedy in the world. Some lines fancifully interpolated by a modern and very inferior hand are here omitted.

V. 122. *And slaided owr the strae.*] The meaning is, *He went hastily over the rank grass.*

V. 144. *As the hip is o the stean.*] This would appear the corruption of some nurse; but taking it as it stands,

stands, the simile, though none of the most delicate, has a parallel in the Father of English Poetry:

> But he was chaste and no lechoure
> And sweet as is the bramble floure
>   That bearethe the red hip.
>
> *Chaucer, Sir Topas.*

ADAM O GORDON.

THE genuine subject of this Ballad has long remained in obscurity, though it must have been noted to every peruser of *Crawford's Memoirs*.

'But to return to Gordon,' (*viz.* Sir Adam Gordon of Auchindown, brother to the Earl of Huntly) 'as
' these two actions against Forbes, or to speak more
' properly, against the rebels, gained him a vast repu-
' tation—his next exploit was attended with an equal
' portion of infamy; and he was as much decryed for
' this unlucky action (though at the same time he had
' no immediate hand in the matter) as for his former
' ones he had been applauded. He had sent one *Captain
' Ker* with a party of foot to summon the Castle of
' *Towie* in the Queen's name. The owner Alexander
' Forbes was not then at home, and his lady confiding
' too much in her sex, not only refused to surrender,
' but gave Ker very injurious language; upon which,
'   unreasonably

' unreasonably transported with fury, he ordered his
' men to fire the castle, and barbarously burnt the un-
' fortunate gentlewoman with her whole family, amount-
' ing to thirty-seven persons. Nor was he ever so much
' as cashiered for this inhuman action, which made
' Gordon share both in the scandal and the guilt.' *An.*
1571. *p.* 240. *edit.* 1706.

In this narrative is immediately perceived every leading circumstance in the Ballad. The *Captain Car*, by which name it was distinguished in Dr. Percy's Manuscript, is evidently the *Ker* of Crawford. The House of *Rodes* I have corrected, according to the truth of story, *Towie*. Of which name, I find in *Gordon of Straloch's* map of Aberdeenshire, there were two gentlemen's seats, or castles, in his time, one upon the *Don*, and another upon the *Ythan*. The nearest seat to the latter is that of *Rothy*, which from wrong information may have originally stood in the Ballad, the mistake rising naturally from the vicinity of their situation, and from this have been corrupted to *Rodes*. The courage of this lady, as represented in the Ballad, was equalled by that of the famous Countess of Salisbury, at the siege of Roxborough; and of Ladies Arundel and Banks, in the last civil wars of England. See particularly the *Mercurius Rusticus*, &c. Lond. 1647. Sections V. and XI.

V. 129.

V. 129. *Freits.*] This word fignifies *ill omens;* and fometimes as here *Accidents fupernaturally unlucky.* King James VI. in his *Dæmonologie, MS. pen. Edit.* B. I. *ch.* IIII. *p.* 13. ' But I pray you forget not likeways
' to tell what are the Devill's rudimentis. E. His ru-
' diments I call firft in generall all that quhilk is called
' vulgairelie the vertu of woode, herbe, and ftaine;
' quhilk is ufed by unlawfull charmis without naturall
' caufis. As lykeways all kynd of prattiques, *freitis, or*
' *uther lyk extraordinair actions, quhilk cannot abyde the trew*
' *twiche of naturall raifon.*' It occurs again in the fame fenfe in *p.* 14. *marg. note;* and in *p.* 41. fpeaking of *Sorcerers.* ' And in generall that naime was gevin
' thaime for ufing of fic chairmis and *freitis,* as that
' craft teachis thame.'

SIR HUGH, OR THE JEW'S DAUGHTER,

is compofed of two copies, one publifhed by Dr. Percy, the other in a collection of Scottifh Songs, &c. *Edin.* 1776. The *Mirryland toun* of the former, and *Mirry Linkin* of the latter, evidently fhew that the noted ftory of Hugh of Lincoln is here expreffed.

FLODDEN

FLODDEN FIELD.

THE ſtanzas here given form a complete copy of this exquiſite Dirge. The inimitable beauty of the original induced a variety of verſifiers to mingle ſtanzas of their own compoſure. But it is the painful, though moſt neceſſary duty of an Editor, by the touchſtone of truth, to diſcriminate ſuch droſs from the gold of antiquity.

SIR PATRICK SPENCE

is given from Dr. Percy's Edition, which indeed agrees with the ſtall copies, and the common recitals. I have, however, lent it a few correćtions, where palpable abſurdity ſeemed to require them. The phraſe in v. 25. of ſeeing the old moon *in the arms* of the new is ſtill familiar in Scotland. It means that the opaque part of the moon's diſk caſts a glimmering light, while the illuminated part is waxing; and is to this hour eſteemed to prognoſticate a ſtorm.

LADY

LADY BOTHWELL's LAMENT.

THESE four ftanzas appeared to the Editor to be all that are genuine of this elegy. Many additional ones are to be found in the common copies, which are rejected as of meaner execution. In a quarto manufcript in the Editor's poffeffion, containing a collection of Poems by different hands from the reign of Queen Elizabeth to the end of the laft century, *(p.* 132.) there are two *Balowes* as they are there ftiled, the firft *The Balow, Allan,* the fecond *Palmer's Balow;* this laft is that commonly called Bothwell's Lament, and the three firft ftanzas in this edition are taken from it, as is the laft from *Allan's Balow.* They are injudicioufly mingled in Ramfay's Edition, and feveral ftanzas of his own added; a liberty he ufed much too often in printing ancient Scottifh poems.

EARL OF MURRAY.

V. laft. *Toun.*] This word is often ufed in Scotland to denote only, perhaps, a farm-houfe and office-houfes, or a number of hovels fcattered here and there; and on which the Englifh would not beftow the name of a village.

SIR JAMES THE ROSE,

is given from a modern edition in one sheet 12mo. after the old copy. A renovation of this Ballad, composed of new and improbable circumstances, decked out with scrapes of tragedies, may be found in the Annual Register for 1774, and other collections. *Rose* is an ancient and honourable name in Scotland: *Johannes de Rose* is a witness to the famous Charter of Robert II. testifying his marriage with *Elizabeth More*, as appears in the rare edition of it printed at Paris, 1695, 4to. *p. 15.*

V. 27. *Belted Knights.*] The *belt* was one of the chief marks which distinguished the ancient knight. *To be girt with the belt of knighthood*, often implied the whole attending ceremonies which constituted that order. That of the common knight was of white leather.

LAIRD OF WOODHOUSELIE.

THIS Ballad is now first published. Whether it has any real foundation, the Editor cannot be positive, though it is very likely. There is a *Woodhouselie* nigh Edinburgh, which may possibly be that here meant.

LORD LIVINGSTON

was probably an anceftor of Livingfton Earl of Linlithgow, attainted in 1715. This affecting piece likewife, with the four following, now appears for the firft time.

V. 13. *Suith dreims are fcant.*] This feems a proverbial expreffion: King James in his *Dæmonologie,* ' That ' is *a fuith dream* (as they fay) fence thay fee it walking.' *MS. p.* 100.

BINNORIE.

V. 32. *Her wraith.*] ' And what meanis then thefe ' kyndis of fpreitis when thay appeare in the fhaddow ' of a perfonne newlie dead, or to die, to his friend ? ' E. When thay appeare upon that occafion, thay are ' called *wraithis* in our langage.' *Ib. p.* 81.

DEATH OF MENTEITH.

WHETHER the *Menteith* in this Ballad is the fame with him, who is reported to have betrayed Wallace, is left in obfcurity.

LORD AIRTH's COMPLAINT.

THESE verses, though somewhat uncouth, are moving, as they seem to flow from the heart. They are now first published from the Editor's quarto Manuscript, *p.* 16. corrected in some lines, which appeared too innacurate for the publick eye. Two entire stanzas are rejected from the same cause. I know nothing of the nobleman to whom they are ascribed.

In the same Manuscript (*p.* 17, and 116.) are to be found the two following Poems, which I believe have never been in print. They are here added, with a few corrections. They were both written by Sir Robert Aytoun, Secretary of State during part of the reigns of William and Mary, and Queen Ann.

SONNET.

SONNET.

WILT thou, remorfelefs fair, ftill laugh while I lament?
Shall ftill thy chief contentment be to fee'me malcontent?
Shall I, Narciffus like, a flying fhadow chafe?
Or, like Pygmalion, love a ftone crown'd with a winning face?
No, know my blind Love now fhall follow Reafon's eyes;
And as thy fairnefs made me fond, thy temper make me wife.
My loyalty difdains to love a lovelefs dame,
The fpirit ftill of Cupid's fire confifts in mutual flame.
Hadft thou but given one look, or hadft thou given one fmile,
Or hadft thou lent but one poor figh my forrows to beguile,
My captive Thoughts perchance had been redeem'd from Pain,
And thefe my mutinous Difcontents made friends with Hope again.
But thou I know at length art carelefs of my good;
And wouldft ambitioufly embrew thy beauty in my blood:
A great difgrace to thee, to me a monftrous wrong,
Which time may teach thee to repent ere haply it be long:
But to prevent thy fhame, and to abridge my woe,
Becaufe thou canft not love thy friend, I'll ceafe to love my foe.

SONG.

SONG.

WHAT means this strangeness now of late,
  Since Time must Truth approve?
This distance may consist with state,
  It cannot stand with love.

'Tis either cunning or distrust
  That may such ways allow:
The first is base, the last unjust;
  Let neither blemish you.

For if you mean to draw me on,
  There needs not half this art:
And if you mean to have me gone,
  You over-act your part.

If kindness cross your wish'd content,
  Dismiss me with a frown;
I'll give you all the love that's spent,
  The rest shall be my own.

FRAGMENTS.

FRAGMENTS.

THE three firſt of theſe are given from a Collection publiſhed at Edinburgh in 1776, but poliſhed by the preſent Editor; the two others from recital. The firſt is a pretty picture of the Fairy court according to the popular notion. I cannot give a better comment on it than in the words of a royal author often before quoted. MS. Dæmonologie, B. III. ch. 5.

Argument.

'The deſcription of the fourth kynde of Spreittis, called the *Pharie*. What is poſſible thairin, and what is but illuſions. Whow far this dialoge entreates of all thir thingis: and to what ende.'

' P. Now I pray you come on to that fourt kynd of
' ſpreittis. *E.* That fourt kynde of Spreitis, quhilk be
' the gentiles was called Diana and her wandring court,
' and amongs us was called the *Pharie* (as I tolde you)
' or our guid neighbouris' (the King has added on the
margin ' or fillie wightis') ' was ane of the ſortis of
' illuſions that was ryfeſt in tyme of Papiſtrie; for all-
' though it was holdin odious to prophefie be the devill,
' yet whome theſe kynd of ſpreittis caried away, and
' informed, thay wer thought to be foncieſt, and of
' beſt

'best lyfe. To speak of the manie vaine tratlis foundit
' upon that illusion; how thair was ane king and queine
' of *Pharie*, of sic a jolie court and traine as thay had;
' how thay had a teind and a dewtie, as it wer, of all
' guidis: how thay naturallie raid and yeid, eat and
' drank, and did all other actions lyke naturall men and
' wemen; I think it is lyker Virgilis *Campi Elisei*, nor
' any thing that aught to be beleived be Chriftianis.'

This Manuscript is wrote in a beautiful Italic hand, so nearly resembling copper-plate engraving, as to have been taken for such even after accurate examination. It is bound in gilded vellum, stamped with the King's cypher beneath the crown; and is in all probability the original copy of this royal monument of superstition. Many additions are inserted on the margin, as would seem, of the hand writing of James VI. and some notes for his own private use. As for instance on *B*. II. *ch*. 1. speaking of the Magicians of his time, over against the words 'Thay are sume of thame riche and worldlie
' wyse,' he has noted *F. M.* ' sum of tham fat or cor-
' pulent in their bodies,' *R. G.* ' and maist pairt of
' thame altogethir gevin ouer to the pleafours of the
' flesche,' *P. N.*

We need not wonder at the severity with which the imaginary crime of witchcraft was punished in his reign, when we remark his sentiment expressed on this head, in *F*. III. *ch*. 6. of this singular tract. '*P*. Then
' to

'to make ane ende of our conference fence I fee it
'drawis leatt, what forme of punifhment think ye
'merites thir Magiciens and Witches? For I fee that
'ye account thame to be all alyke giltie. E. (*The King*)
'*Thay aught to be put to deathe*, according to the law of
'God, the civill and imperiall law, and the municipal
'law of all Chriftiane nations. *P*. But what kynde of
'death I pray you? *E*. It is commonlie ufed be fyre,
'but that is ane indifferent thing to be ufed in every
'cuntrey according to the law or cuftume thairof. *P.*
'*But aught no fexe, aage, nor rank, to be eximed?* E.
' NONE AT ALL.'

The language of this pedantic Monarch is particular:
it is that of a Scottifh fchool-boy beginning to read
Englifh.

V.

It is furprifing that the exiftence of fuch beings as
men of the fea, and *mermaids*, fhould ftill be queftioned
even by authors of inquiry. So many examples occur
in hiftory natural and political, that it would feem
placed beyond all doubt, if human teftimony may
be in the leaft relied on. The following being very
fingular, and, having efcaped the notice of the late
writers on this fubject, from their being to be found in
an uncommon treatife, it is hoped they will not be un-
acceptable.

' Pendant

' Pendant le séjour que fit à Derbent Salam envoyé
' par Vatec, calife de la race des Abassides vers la mer
' Caspienne, pour reconnoitre l'endroit de la forteresse,
' que les anciens disent avoir été bâtie, pour empêcher
' les peuples du Nord de faire des courses, il arriva un
' fait singulier. Je le tire de Casvini, auteur Arabe, qui
' dans son livre intitulé, *Aganb el Makloukat*, c'est à dire,
' des choses merveilleuses qui se font trouvées dans les
' créatures, le place à l'an de l'Egire 288, qui repond
' à l'année 894 de notre ére. Il rapporte que le Prince
' de ce pays-la allant un jour à la pêche sur la mer Cas-
' pienne, mena avec lui Salam. On prit dans cette
' pêche un fort grand poisson, qu'on ouvrit sur le champ,
' et dans le ventre duquel on trouva une fille marine en-
' core vivante. Elle étoit ceinte d'une caleçon sans cou-
' ture fait d'une peau semblable à celle de l'homme,
' qui lui descendoit jusqu' aux genoux. Cette fille avoit
' les mains sur son visage, et s'arrachoit les cheveux.
' Elle poussoit des grands soupirs, et ne vêcut que peu
' de momens apres avoir été tirée du ventre de ce mon-
' stre. Casvini adjoute, que le *Tarik Magreb*, Histoire
' Arabe d'Afrique, confirme cette narration par d' au-
' tres faits, qu'il cite au sujet des Sirênes, et des Tri-
' tons trouvés dans le mer.

' Voici un autre fait, tiré d'un procès verbal, dressé
' par Pierre Luce Sr. de la Paire, capitan commandant
' les quartiers du Diamant à la Martinique le 31 Mai,
' 1671,

NOTES. 123

‘ 1671, reçu par Pierre de Beville notaire des quartiers
‘ de fa compagnie, en prefence du Pere Julien Simon
‘ jéfuite, et des trois autres témoins, qui ont figné au
‘ procès verbal, contenant les depofitions feparées et
‘ unanimes de deux François, et quatre negres. Cet
‘ Acte porte, que le 23 du meme mois du Mai, ces
‘ François et ces Negres etant allés le matin aux ifles du
‘ Diamant avec un bateau pour pêcher, et voulant s'en
‘ revenir vers le coucher du Soleil, ils apperçurent près
‘ du bord d'une petite ifle ou ils etoient, un monftre
‘ marin ayant la figure humain de la ceinture en haut,
‘ et ce terminant par le bas en poiffon. Sa queue etoit
‘ large, et fendue comme celle d'une Carrangue, poif-
‘ fon fort commun dans cette mer. Il avoit la tête de
‘ la groffeur et de la forme de celle d'un homme ordi-
‘ naire, avec des cheveux unis, noirs mêlés de gris, qui
‘ lui pendoit fur les épaules ; le vifage large et plein, le
‘ nez gros et camus, les yeux de forme accoutumée,
‘ les oreilles larges ; une barbe de même, pendante de
‘ fept à huit pouces, et mêlée de gris comme les che-
‘ veux ; l'eftomac couvert de poil de la même couleur ;
‘ les bras et les mains femblables aux notres avec lef-
‘ quelles (lofqu'il fortoit de l'eau, ce qu'il fit deux
‘ fois, en plongeant et s'approchant toujours du rivage
‘ de l'Ifle) il paroiffoit s'effuyer le vifage, en les y por-
‘ tant à plufieurs reprifes, et reniflant au fortir de l'eau,
‘ comme font les chiens barbets. Le corps qui s'ele-
‘ voit

' voit au deſſus de l'eau juſqu' à la ceinture, étoit dé-
' liè comme celui d'un jeune homme de quinze à ſeix
' ans, il avoit la peau mediocrement blanche; et la
' longueur de tout le corps paroiſſoit être d'environ
' cinq pieds.' &c. Telliamed, *ou Entretiens d'un Phi-
loſophe Indien*, &c. *par M. de Maille*, Amſt. 1748, *tom*. II.
p. 152. 154. Many accounts of equal curioſity, and
as well vouched, may be found in the ſame volume;
but I queſtion much if the ſtory of the Engliſh ſhip
belonging to *Hall* (perhaps we ſhould read *Hull*) be
properly authenticated.

GLOSSARY.

GLOSSARY.

A

Ablins, *perhaps*.
Aboon, *above*.
Ae, ane, *one*.
Aff, *off*.
Aft, *oft*.
Aith, *oath*.
Ain, *own*.
Alfe, *except*.
Anes, *once*.
Auld, *old*.
Aufterne, *ftern*.
Ayont, *beyond*.

B

Ba, *ball, tennis*.
Baird, *beard*.
Baith, *both*.
Bairn, *child*.
Bale, *mifery*.
Balow, *hufh*.
Band, *folemn oath*.
Bafe-court, *bas court*, French, *the lower court of a caftle*.
Bafnet, *helmet*.
Begyle, *beguile*.
Beftraught, *diftracted*.
Bunfters, *blufterers*.
Beik, *bafk*.

Belyve, *immediately*.
Belprent, *covered*.
Betide, n. *fortune*.
Bedeen, *prefently*.
Bleife, *blaze*.
Bleirit, *dim with tears*.
Blink, *glimpfe of light*.
Blinking, *twinkling*.
Blude, *blood*.
Blythfum, *fprightly*.
Boughts, *fheepfolds*.
Boift, *boaft*.
Bonny, *pretty*.
Botand, *likeways*.
Bown, *make ready*.
Bogle, *hobgoblin*.
Bot, *without*.
Bouir, *a room arched in the Gothic manner*.
Bouir woman, *chamber maid*.
Bra, *bravely dreffed*.
Brae, *fide of a hill*.
Braid, *broad*.
Brand, Ifl. *a fword*.
Brawe, *brave*.
Brayd, *haften*.
Bruik, *enjoy*.
Brin, *burn*.

Brig.

Brig, *bridge.*
Bufk, *prepare.*

C
Cauld, *cold.*
Cauldrif, *chill, damp.*
Canny, *prudent.*
Cheis, *chufe.*
Claught, *grafped.*
Cliding, *wardrobe.*

D
Daffin, *waggery.*
Dar'd, *lighted, hit.*
Darrain, *fuffer, encounter.*
Deft, *taken off haftily.*
Dint, *blow, ftroke.*
Dawning, *dawn of day.*
Dought, *could.*
Doughty, *valiant, ftrong.*
Dowie, *dreadfull, melancholy.*
Drie, *fuffer, endure.*
Dule, *grief.*

E
Eard, *earth.*
Eild, *eld, old age*
Eine, *eyes.*
Eithly, *eafily.*
Eydent, *ayding, affifting.*
Elric, *difmal.*
Eldern, *ancient, venerable.*
Egre, *eager, keen, fharp.*
Effray, *affright.*
Emraud, *Emerald.*

Ettle, *aim.*
Ezar? *This word occurs in Spenfer.*

F
Fae, *foe.*
Fay, *faith, fincerity.*
Fere, *companion.*
Ferly, *wonder.*
Feid, *enmity.*
Fey, *in footh.*
Flinders. *fplinters.*
Fleeching, *flattering.*
Forbere, *forefather, anceftor.*
Forbode, *denial.*
Frae, *fro, from.*
Frawart, *froward.*

G
Ga, gae, gang, *gô.*
Gabbing, *prattle.*
Gait, *way, path.*
Gar, *caufe.*
Gie, *give.*
Gin, *gif, if.*
Glaive, *fword.*
Gleit, *glittered.*
Glie, *mirth.* In H. P. II. 120. *it feems to fignify a faint light.*
Glent, *glanced.*
Glift, *gliftered.*
Gloming, *dufk.*
Glowr, *glare, difmal light.*
Grein, *defire.*
Greit, *weep.*

Graith,

GLOSSARY.

Graith, *dress*, v. and n.
Gousty, *ghastly.*
Grie, *prize, victory.*
Gude, *good.*
Gurly, *bitter, cold; applied to weather.*
Gyle, *guile.*
Gyse, *manner, fashion.*

H

Harst, *harvest.*
Hauld, *hold, abode.*
Hain, *spare, save.*
Hap, *cover.*
Hecht, *promised.*
Hip, *the berry of the wild rose.*
Hyt, *frantic.*
Hynd, *hence.*

I

Jimp, *delicate, slender.*
Ilk, ilka; *each.*
Irie, *terrible.*

K

Kaming, *combing.*
Kin, *kindred.*
Kyth, v. *to show or make appear.*
Kyth, n. *acquaintance, friends, companions.*

L

Laigh, *low.*
Lane, *alone.*

Lap, *leaped.*
Law, *low.*
Lave, *the rest.*
Leil, *true, faithful.*
Leir, *learn.*
Leglen, *a milking pail.*
Leman, *lover, mistress.*
Leugh, *laughed.*
Lawing, *reckoning.*
Lever, *rather.*
Leech, *physician.*
Lift, *the firmament.*
Lig, *lye scatteredly.*
Lilting, *merry making with music, &c.*
Lin, *a fall of water.*
Linkis, *lamps, or other artificial lights.*
Loaning, *a common green near a village.*
Loch, *lake.*
Low, v. and n. *flame.*
Lown, *sheltered, calm.*
Lout, *to bow.*
Lue, *love.*
Lure, *cunning device, snare.*
Lyart, *hoary.*

M

Makless, *matchless.*
Maun, *must.*
Mair, *more f. rather.*
Mahoun, *Mahomet, and by abuse the devil.*
Mane, *moan, lament.*
Meikle, *much.*

Meiny,

GLOSSARY

Meiny, *train, army.*
Mense, *to measure, to try.*
Mede, *reward.*
Meid, *port, appearance.*
Meise, *soften, mollify.*
Mirk, *dark.*
Mony, *many.*
Mote, *might.*

N
Na, nae, *no, none.*
Neist, *next.*
Norse, *often the King of Norway, so France is often used by Shakspeare for the king of that country.*

O
On case, *perhaps.*
Ony, *any.*
Or, *s. ere, before, s. else.*
Owr, *Over.*
Outowr, *Over above.*
Orison, *Fr. prayer.*

P
Pall, *robe of state.*
Payne, *penalty.*
Perle, *pearl.*
Pleasance, *pleasure.*
Pou, *pull.*
Pratique, *experiment.*
Preass, *to press, to pass with difficulty.*
Prime of day, *dawn.*

Prive, pruve, *prove.*
Propine, *reward.*

Q
Qu, *is used in old Scottish spelling for W. as* Quhut, *What,* &c.
Quat, *quitted.*
Quell, *subdue.*

R
Raught, recht, *reached.*
Recule, *recoil.*
Rede, *warn.*
Reiking, *smoking.*
Rief, *robbery.*
Riever, *robber.*
Reid, *red.*
Roun, *sound softly, whispers*
Rue, *repent.*
Ruth, *pity.*
Rude, *cross.*
Runkled, *wrinkled.*

S
Sark, *shirt.*
Saw, *a wise saying.*
Sawman, *counsellor.*
Sabbing, *sobbing.*
Scant, *scarce.*
Scorning (Flod. v. 5.) *jesting ironically.*
Sey, *essay, try.*
Seen, *to see.*
Seim, *appearance.*
Selcouth,

GLOSSARY.

Selcouth, *uncommon as a prodigy.*
Share, *to cleave, pierce.*
Shathmont?
Sic, *such.*
Sindle, *seldom.*
Skaith, *hurt.*
Slaid, *to move speedily.*
Slee, v. *slay.*
Sen, *seeing.*
Sin, sith, *since.*
Soncie, *lucky.*
Stalwart, *stout, valiant.*
Steik, *to shut.*
Sleuth, *sloth.*
Strecht, *stretched.*
Swankies, *merry fellows.*
Swaird, *turf, grassy ground.*
Swith, *quickly.*
Steid, *estate.*
Splent, *armour for the thighs and legs.*
Speir, *ask.*
Stoup, *pillar.*
Sucred, *sugared.*
Syre, *lord.*

T

Tane, *taken.*
Targe, *shield.*
Tein, *sorrow.*
Teind, *tyth, tenth part.*
Thilk, thir, *these.*
Thole, *suffer, permit.*
Thud, *sudden noise.*

Tide, *time, season.*
Tint, *lost.*
Triest, *make an assignation.*
Twin'd, *parted, separated.*

V U

Veir, *avoid,* or perhaps *alter,*
Unmusit, *without wonder;* to muse *often means to* wonder *in Shakspeare.*
Unsonsie, *unlucky.*

W

Waddin, *strong, firm.*
Wad, wald, wold; *would.*
Warloc, *wizard.*
Wallow, *withered,* and fig. *pale.*
Ward, *sentinel.*
Wate, *warrand.*
Wax, *to spread, to become famous.*
Wee, *little.*
Weit, *wet, rain.*
Wete, *hope.*
Westlin, *western.*
Wae worth ye, *woe befall you.*
War, *aware.*
Whilk, *which.*
Wighty, *strong.*
Wicht, *from* Wiga Sax. *a hero, or great man.*
Winsum, *agreeable, winning.*
Whyle, *until.*

K   Weir,

Weir, *war*.
Weily, *full of whirlpools; a weil is still used for a whirlpool in the west of Scotland.*
Wraith, *a spirit or ghost.*
Wyte, *blame.*
Wreak, *revenge.*
Wreken, *avenged.*

Wreuch, *grief, misery.*

Y

Yestreen, *the evening of yesterday.*
Yet, *gate.*
Yied, *went.*
Youthheid, *state of youth.*

THE END.

www.ingramcontent.com/pod-product-compliance
Lightning Source LLC
Chambersburg PA
CBHW030253170426
43202CB00009B/731